Alphonse Lee Rymer

Normal Outlines of General History

Alphonse Lee Rymer

Normal Outlines of General History

ISBN/EAN: 9783741187551

Manufactured in Europe, USA, Canada, Australia, Japa

Cover: Foto ©ninafisch / pixelio.de

Manufactured and distributed by brebook publishing software (www.brebook.com)

Alphonse Lee Rymer

Normal Outlines of General History

NORMAL OUTLINES
✦ OF ✦
GENERAL HISTORY

TABLES OF GREAT MEN OF CENTURIES

HISTORICAL SAYINGS AND PSEUDONYMS

Questions and Answers

By A. L. RYMER

CHARLESTON, W. VA.
THE TRIBUNE COMPANY
1898

COPYRIGHTED
by
A. L. RYMER.

Preface.

The plan of these Outlines of General History has been so adapted that they may be used with any text-books, and much information might be obtained from them alone.

The author has felt the need of just such a work in the school room, and these outlines are the result of his experience in teaching the subject.

I do not claim originality (and who does in history) in anything except the arrangement, and I would be willing to credit all those who so desire with some shares of stock in this feature.

In the tables, Great Men of Centuries, Pseudonyms and Sayings, and others, do not expect to find completeness; but only a *guide* for more complete work. For elementary work, they are probably full enough.

Especial attention is directed to the arrangement of the *questions and answers.* Many "Quiz Books" are objectionable because they do not train mind action, but depend upon the memory altogether; and a question may be as different in relation to the proceeding one as a simoom is different from a monsoon. This objection is met (I hope) by grouping the questions under designated headings, and placing them in chronological order. In this manner, one question leads to another one, often on the same subject, and we proceed from the "known to the related unknown," and by means of association review history systematically.

England is treated of more fully because of its historical nearness to us, and the United States is purposely omitted, for the reason that every student of General History is supposed to be well versed in the history of his own country.

A. L. R.

Buffalo, W. Va., May 3, 1897.

Table of Contents.

Chapter I—Races 9
Chapter II—Divisions of History 10
Chapter III—Egypt 11
Chapter IV—Babylonia-Assyria 13
Chapter V—Judea 15
Chapter VI—China and India 18
Chapter VII—Phoenicia 19
Chapter VIII—Medo-Persia 20
Chapter IX—Greece 24
Chapter X—Rome 32
Chapter XI—Mediaeval History 43
Chapter XII—Modern History 56
Chapter XIII—Chas. V. and Reformation 57
Chapter XIV—Rise of the Dutch Republic 58
Chapter XV—Wars of France 58
Chapter XVI—England under the Tudors 59
Chapter XVII—The Thirty Years War 61
Chapter XVIII—Monarchy in France 62
Chapter XIX—England under the Stuarts 63

Chapter XX—Peter the Great and Charles XII........ 65
Chapter XXI—Rise of Prussia...................... 66
Chapter XXII—England under House of Hanover.... 67
Chapter XXIII—French Revolution and France....... 67
Chapter XXIV—England in the 19th Century......... 71
Chapter XXV—Other Modern Nations............... 72
Chapter XXVI—Great Men of Centuries.........31-40-52
Chapter XXVII—Pseudonyms and Sayings........... 84
Chapter XXVIII—Creasy's Decisive Battles.......... 90

Appendix.

Chapter XXIX—Questions on Ancient History....... 91
Chapter XXX—Questions on Mediaeval History...... 94
Chapter XXXI—Questions on Modern History....... 96
Chapter XXXII—Answers to Questions on Ancient History............................100
Chapter XXXIII—Answers to Questions on Mediaeval History........................108
Chapter XXXIV—Answers to Questions on Modern History..........................115

Outlines of General History.

Chapter I.—Races of Mankind.

I. **Black Race.**
- 1. Negroes.
- 2. Australians.

II. **Yellow Race.**
- 1. Chinese.
- 2. Burmese.
- 3. Tartars.
- 4. Mongols.
- 5. Turks.
- 6. Huns.
- 7. Finns.
- 8. Esquimaux.
- 9. Malays. †
- 10. Indians. (Amer.) ‡

III. **White Race.**
- 1. Semitic Family. (Descendants of Shem).
  - 1. Chaldeans. *
  - 2. Assyrians.
  - 3. Babylonians.
  - 4. Canaanites (chiefly).
  - 5. Phoenicians.
  - 6. Hebrews.
  - 7. Arabs.
- 2. Hamitic Family. (Descendants of Ham.)
  - 1. Egyptians.
  - 2. Libyans.
  - 3. Cushites.
- 3. Aryan Family.
  - 1. Indo-Iranic Branch.
    - 1. Hindoos.
    - 2. Medes.
    - 3. Persians.
  - 2. Græco-Italic Branch.
    - 1. Greeks.
    - 2. Romans.

† Classed as a separate race by some authors. ‡ Also known as Indian or Red Race.
* Partly Semitic.

10   OUTLINES OF GENERAL HISTORY

III. WHITE RACE.—Cont'd. (Descendants of Japheth.)
- 3. Celtic Branch.
  - 1. Picts.
  - 2. Scotts.
  - 3. Britons.
  - 4. Gauls.
- 4. Teutonic Branch.
  - 1. Scandinavians.
  - 2. Germans.
- 5. Slavonic Branch.
  - 1. Russians.
  - 2. Poles.

Chapter II.—Divisions of History.

I. ANCIENT HISTORY.
1. Date—From the Earliest times to 476 A. D.
2. Countries.
   1. Egypt.
   2. Babylonia-Assyria.
   3. Judea.
   4. China and India.
   5. Phœnicia.
   6. Medo-Persia.
   7. Greece.
   8. Rome.

II. MEDIÆVAL HISTORY.
1. Date.
   1. Dark Ages. From 476 A. D. to 1100 A. D.
   2. Dawn. From 1100 A. D. to 1500 A. D.
2. Topics.
   1. The Teutons.
   2. Byzanitum.
   3. Mohammedanism.
   4. Charlemagne.
   5. The Crusaders.
   6. The 100 Years War.
   7. War of the Roses.
   8. Rise of Mod'n Nations.
   9. Great Men.

OUTLINES OF GENERAL HISTORY 11

III. MODERN HISTORY.
- 1. Date—From 1500 to the Present Time.
- 2. Important Events of
  - 1. The 16th Century.
  - 2. The 17th Century.
  - 3. The 18th Century.
  - 5. The 19th Century.
  - 5. Great Men.

Chapter III.—Egypt.

I. GEOGRAPHICAL DIVISIONS.
1. Upper Egypt.
2. Middle Egypt.
3. Lower Egypt.

II. LOCATION AND SIZE.
1. On the Nile in Eastern Africa.
2. It is as large as Georgia.

III. POLITICAL HISTORY.

1. The Old Empire 3700 B. C. to 1900 B. C.
   1. Pyramids built at Gizeh in 4th Dynasty.
   2. Organization of Military Service.
   3. Memphis Supplanted by Thebes in the 11th Dynasty.
   4. War with Ethiopians.
   5. Conquered by the Hyksos.

2. The Middle Empire 1900 B. C. to 1525 B. C.
   1. Rule of the "Shepherd Kings".
   2. Thotmes III. drives off the Hyksos and becomes King.

12   OUTLINES OF GENERAL HISTORY

		3. The New Empire 1525 B. C. to 525 B.C.	1. Her Great Glory.
			2. Conquered by Persia.
			3. Its Decline.

IV. NOTED MEN.
  1. Rulers.
    1. Amosis.
    2. Khufu.
    3. Rameses II.
    4. Thotmes III.
    5. Menepthah.
    6. Necho.
  2. Joseph.

V. CIVILIZATION.
  1. Classes of People.
    1. Priests.
    2. Soldiers.
    3. Lower Classes.
  2. They had reverence for their kings.
  3. Noted on account of
    1. Pyramids.
    2. Obelisks.
    3. Sphinxes.
    4. Statues.
    5. Hieroglyphics.
    6. Mummies.
  4. The People were
    1. Weavers.
    2. Dyers.
    3. Miners of Precious Ores.
    4. Manufacturers of Glass.
    5. Potters.
    6. Mathematicians.
    7. Astronomers.
  5. Their Literature
    1. Was chiefly Religious.
    2. Written on Papyrus Scrolls.
    3. Phatokep's "Book of the Dead"—chief work.
  6. Religion. Consisted of
    1. Belief in an Invisible God.
    2. Triads

V. CIVILIZATION.—
Continued.
- 6. Religion.
  - 1. Consisted of
    - 1. Consisted like
      - 1. Osiris—husband.
      - 2. Isis—wife.
      - 3. Horus—son.
    - 3. Planets.
    - 4. Worship of Animals.
      - 1. Cats.
      - 2. Goats.
      - 3. Bulls.
      - 4. Sheep
      - 5. Crocodiles.
  - 2. Character—Superstitious in the extreme.
- 7. Education—priestly.

Chapter IV.—(2) Babylonia-Assyria.

I. GEOGRAPHICAL DIVISIONS.
1. Chaldea.
2. Shinar.
3. Mesopotamia.
4. Babylonia.
5. Assyria.
6. Armenia.

II. LOCATION AND SIZE.
1. In South-western Asia.
2. Extent—From the Mediterranean Sea to the Caspian and from the Taurus Mountains to Egypt and the Persian Gulf.
3. About five times as large as Texas.

III. POLITICAL HISTORY.
1. Chaldean Supremacy (4000 B. C. to 1250 B. C.
   1. Nimrod founds Babylon.
   2. Sargon I.
   3. Uruch, King of Ur.
   4. Rise of Assyria.

14   OUTLINES OF GENERAL HISTORY

III. POLITICAL HISTORY.—Cont'd.

2. Assyrian Supremacy, (1250 B.C. to 625 B.C.)
  1. Important Kings.
    1. Tiglathinin.
    2. Tiglath-Pileser I
    3. Sardanapalus II.
    4. Shalamanezer II.
    5. Tiglath— Pileser II.
    6. Sennecharib.
    7. Esarhaddon.
    8. Necho.
  2. Fall of Nineveh—625 B. C.

3. Babylonian Supremacy, (625 B. C. to 538 B. C.)
  1. Its Kings.
    1. Nabopolassar.
    2. Nebuchednezzar.
    3. Nabonadius.
    4. Belshazzar.
  2. Babylon Conquered by Persians 538 B. C.

IV. CIVILIZATION.

1. Were noted because
  1. Studied the Heavenly Bod's
  2. Divided the year into days and hours.

1. These people were noted because they
  3. Named the Stars.
  4. Described the Zodiac.
  5. Observed Eclipses.
  6. Built canals, aqueducts and Palaces.
  7. Erected Aquariums and Hanging Gardens.
  8. Made Gold, Silver and Bronze Vases.
  9. Made Woven Stuffs.
  10. Used Transparent and Painted Glass.
  11. Buried their dead in Honey and Clay Jars.
  12. Married their Daughters at Auction.

IV. CIVILIZATION.—Continued.

- 2. Their Literature.
  - 1. Was written in Cuneiform characters on pillow-shaped Tablets and Cylinders.
  - 2. And they had a Library of Clay Books on
    1. Law.
    2. History.
    3. Mathematics.
    4. Botany.
    5. Astronomy.
    6. Zoology.
    7. Astrology.
    8. Religion.
- 3. Religion
  - 1. Consisted of
    1. *Il.* or *Ra.*—Chief God.
    2. First Triads.
       1. Ana—Chaotic Spirit.
       2. Bel—Hunter.
       3. Hoa—Lord of the Abyss.
    3. Other Triad as
       1. Sin—Moon God.
       2. San—Sun God.
       3. Vul—Air God.
    4. Planetary Deties as
       1. Saturn.
       2. Jupiter.
       3. Mars, etc.
  - 2. Character Idolatrous.

Chapter V.—(3) Judea.

I. TRIBAL DIVISIONS.
1. Simon.
2. Judah.
3. Dan.
4. Benjamin.
5. Manasseh.
6. Gad.
7. Reuben.
8. Asher.
9. Zebulun.
10. Naphtali.
11. Levi.
12. Joseph.

16   OUTLINES OF GENERAL HISTORY

II. LOCATION AND SIZE.
- 1. Situate on East of the Red Sea, South of the Mediterranean Sea.
- 2. About one-third as large as West Virginia.

III. POLITICAL HISTORY.

1. Patriarchal Age. (2000 B. C. to 1491 B. C.)
  - 1. Great Men.
    - 1. Abraham.
    - 2. Isaac.
    - 3. Jacob.
    - 4. Moses.
  - 2. The Bondage in Egypt.
  - 3. The Exodus 1491 B. C.

2. Age of the Judges (1491 B. C. to 1095 B. C.)
  - 1. Military Chiefs.
    - 1. Moses.
    - 2. Joshua.
  - 2. Judges.
    - 1. Othniel.
    - 2. Ehud.
    - 3. Shagmar.
    - 4. Deborah and Balak.
    - 5. Gideon.
    - 6. Abimelech.
    - 7. Tolah.
    - 8. Jair.
    - 9. Jepthah.
    - 10. Ibzan.
    - 11. Elon.
    - 12. Abdon.
    - 13. Eli.
    - 14. Samson.
    - 15. Samuel.
  - 3. Conquest of Palestine.

3. The Monarchy. (1095 B. C. to 975 B. C.)
  - 1. Its Kings
    - 1. Saul, 40 yrs.
    - 2. David, 40 yrs.
    - 3. Solomon, 40 yrs.
  - 2. Division in 975 B. C.

III. POLITICAL HISTORY. Cont'd.

- 4. Monarchy Divided.
  - 1. Israel (the 10 tribes). (975 B. C. to 722 B. C.
    - 1. Jeroboam as King.
    - 2. Capital—Samaria.
    - 3. Their Captivity.
    - 4. Daniel.
    - 5. Hospitality of Cyrus.
  - 2. Judah, Tribes of Judah and Benjamin. (975 B. C. to 586 B. C.
    - 1. Rehoboam as King.
    - 2. Capital—Jerusalem.
    - 3. Zedekiah—last King.
    - 4. Captivity.
    - 5. Summary.

IV. CIVILIZATION.

- 1. Noted because they
  - 1. Were Farmers.
  - 2. Gave us Christian and Jewish Religions.
  - 3. Used the Mosaic Laws.
  - 4. Compelled every boy to learn a trade.
  - 5. Had the first Republic.
- 2. Literature.
  - 1. Books.
    - 1. Bible.
    - 2. The Talmud.
  - 2. Writings of
    - 1. Philo.
    - 2. Josephus.
- 3. Education.
  - 1. Compulsory.
  - 2. Theocratic.

Chapter VI.—(4) China and India.

I. LOCATION AND SIZE.
1. China is in Eastern and Middle Asia.
2. Her territory is about one-half as large as all the United States.
3. India is South and West of China and same size.

II. POLITICAL HISTORY.
1. General Nature.
   1. Isolated from other countries.
   2. Little known until about 500 B. C.
2. Chronology.
   1. Earliest date of Turanians in China, 3000 B. C.
   2. India's History begins about 1500 B. C.
   3. Migration of Aryans.
   4. Age of Confucius in China, 551 to 478 B. C.
   5. Buddha in India, 500 B. C.
   6. Alexander's Invasion of India, 327 B. C.
   7. Age of Mencius, 300 B. C.
   9. Chewangte Emperor of China, 246 B. C. to 210 B. C.
   9. Building of the Great Wall, 215 B. C. to 204 B. C.

III. CIVILIZATION.
1. India had commercial relations with Italian cities and Greece and Rome.
2. Chinese policy was, *no intercourse.*
3. They reverenced their ancestors.
4. Made memory a test of education.
5. Taught the 9 Classics in China and Castes in India.

III. CIVILI-ZATION. Cont'd.
- 6. Religion.
  - 1. Kinds.
    - 1. In China.
      - 1. Confucianism.
      - 2. Taoism.
    - 2. In India—Brahmanism.
    - 3. In both—Buddhism.
  - 2. Books.
    - 1. Vedas or Hymns.
    - 2. Books of Confucius.

Chapter VII.—(5) Phoenicia.

I. LOCATION AND SIZE.
- 1. Situate, midway between the East & West
- 2. Area, about 2200 square miles.
- 3. Important Colonies.
  - 1. Cadiz, in Spain.
  - 2. Utica and
  - 3. Carthage. } in Africa.
  - 4. The Islands of
    - 1. Cyprus.
    - 2. Sicily.
    - 3. Sardinia.

II. POLITICAL HISTORY.
- 1. Sidonian Supremacy. (1550 B. C. to 1100 B. C.)
  - 1. Sidon founded, 1550 B. C.
  - 2. It becomes the Capital.
  - 3. Tyre founded about 1150 B. C.
  - 4. Rise of Tyre, 1100 B. C.
- 2. Tyrian Supremacy. (1100 B. C. to 850 B. C.)
  - 1. Hiram builds Temples 1025 B. C.
  - 2. Carthage founded 880 B. C.
  - 3. Its capture by the Assyrians 850 B. C.
- 3. Foreign Supremacy.
  - 1. Under Assyrians.
  - 2. Nebuchednezzar takes Tyre, 585 B. C.
  - 3. Alexander takes Tyre, 332 B. C.
  - 4. Roman conquest.

III. CIVILI-
ZATION.
- 1. Noted because they
  1. Gave us the alphabet.
  2. Observed effect of Moon on Tides.
  3. Were Commercial Traders.
  4. Good Carpenters and Engravers.
  5. Excellent farm's and miners.
  6. Worked in { 1. Ivory. 3. Metal. 2. Pottery. 4. Glass
  7. Used Perfumes and Ornamentals.
- 2. Religion
  1. Similar to the Assyrians.
  2. Except { 1. They sacrificed human beings. 2. And worshiped the Gods of { 1. Baal. 2. Moloch.
  3. Character Idolatrous

Chapter VIII.—(6) Medo-Persia.

I. LOCATION AND SIZE.
1. East of Babylonia.
2. Extent, from the Caspian Sea and Parthia and from the Persian Gulf to the Caucasus Mts.
3. About six times as large as Texas at first, but afterwards became larger.

II. IMPORTANT COLONIAL DIVISIONS.
1. Egypt.
2. Babylonia.
3. Assyria.
4. Lydia.
5. Thrace.
6. Macedonia.
7. Part of Scythia.
8. Ionian Cities.

III. POLITICAL HISTORY.
1. Median Supremacy (625 B. C. to 558 B. C.)
  1. Early History.
  2. Kings. { 1. Cyaxares, 625 B. C. to 585 B. C. 2. Astyages, 585 B. C. to 585 B. C.
  3. Rise of Persia.

- III. Political History —Con't.
  - 2. Persian Supremacy (558 B. C. to 330 B. C.)
    - 1. Cyrus (558 B. C. to 529 B. C.)
      - 1. Overthrow Astyages.
      - 2. Defeats Croesus.
      - 3. Captures Babylon.
      - 4. His Death.
    - 2. Cambyses, (529 to 522 B. C.)
      - 1. Conquers Egypt.
      - 2. The Libyan Expedition.
      - 3. The Smerdis Affair.
    - 3. Darius I. (521 B. C. to 486 B. C.)
      - 1. Capitals
        - 1. Susa.
        - 2. Persepolis.
      - 2. Grecian Wars.
      - 3. His Work.

- III. Political History —Con't.
  - 2. Persian Supremacy (558 B. C. to 330 B. C.)
    - 4. Xerxes I. (486 B. C. to 465 B. C.)
      - 1. Crushes Eastern Revolt.
      - 2. Second War with Greece.
      - 3. His Work.
    - 5. Artaxerxes I. (465 B. C. to 425 B. C.)
      - 1. Decline of the Empire.
      - 2. The 10,000 Greeks.
    - 6. Other Kings.
      - 1. Pseudo-Smerdis, 522 B. C.
      - 2. Xerxes II. 425 B. C.
      - 3. Sogdianus 424 B. C.
      - 4. Darius II. 424 B. C.
      - 5. Artaxerxes II. 405 B. C.
  - 3. Foreign Supremacy.
    - 1. Greece.
    - 2. Rome.

6. Other Kings.
- 6. Artaxerxes III. 359 B. C.
- 7. Arses, 338 B. C.
- 8. Darius III. 336 B.C. to 330 B.C.
  - 1. Alexander's Invasion.
    - 1. Granicus
    - 2. Issus.
    - 3. Arbela.
  - 2. Battles.

IV. CIVILIZATION.

1. Noted because they
   1. Ate but one meal each day.
   2. Drank wine instead of water.
   3. Wrote from left to right.
   4. Wrote on rocks and prepared skins.
   5. Wore massive gold collars, etc.
   6. Plated their tables with gold and silver.
   7. Depended upon numbers in fight.
   8. Emulated the Virtues.
   9. Kept the women in seclusion.
      - 1. Riding.
      - 2. Drawing the Bow.
      - 3. Truth.

2. The Kings.
   1. Had 15,000 servants and more.
   2. A gorgeous court.
   3. Had Spies, called "King's Eyes" and "King's Ears."
   4. Got drunk once each year for public exhibition.

IV. CIVILIZATION. Continued.
- 3. The Soldiers.
  - 1. Infantry.
    - 1. Used bow and arrows, swords, battle axes and slings.
    - 2. Wore leather tunic and trousers, low boots and felt cap.
  - 2. Cavalry.
    - 1. Used leather thongs and javelins.
    - 2. Wore metal coats of mail.
- 4. Their Architecture was placed on Palaces and Tombs.
- 5. Literature.
  - 1. Nature.
  - 2. Book-Zend-Avesta.
- 6. Education.
  - 1. State.
  - 2. Dependence on colonies for manufactures.
- 7. Religion.
  - 1. Zoroastrianism.
    - 1. Founded by Zoroaster.
    - 2. Nature, a dualism observed.
    - 3. Principal Gods.
      - 1. Ormazd— God, Good or Lightness.
      - 2. Ahriman— God of Evil or Darkness.
    - 4. Worshiped both these Gods.

24 OUTLINES OF GENERAL HISTORY

IV. CIVILI-
ZATION.
Continued.
{ 2. Mag-
ianism.
{ 1. Fire.
2. Air.
3. Earth.
4. Water
} All Worshiped.

Chapter IX.—(7) Greece.

I. GEO-
GRAPHICAL
DIVISIONS.

1. Northern Greece.
 1. Districts.
  1. Thessaly.
  2. Epirus.
 2. Mountains.
  1. Olympus.
  2. Ossa and Pelion, (a)
  3. Cambrarian Range.
 3. Oracle of Zeus, (a)

2. Central Greece.
 1. Districts.
  1. Phocis.
  2. Boetia.
  3. Attica and eight others.
 2. Mountains.
  1. Parnassus, (b)
  2. Helicon.
  3. Hymettes.
  4. Pentelicus.
  5. Pindus Range.
 3. Delphian Oracle (b)

3. Southern Greece, (or Peleponnesus).
 1. Districts.
  1. Accaia.
  2. Argolis.
  3. Accadia.
  4. Messenia.
  5. Lacadaemon, and 6 others.
 2. Very Mountainous.

II. LOCATION AND SIZE—Directly East of N. Y. and same size

III. PRINCIPAL ISLANDS.
1. Delos.
2. Cyclades.
3. Ionian Islands.
4. Euboa.
5. Corcyra.
6. Ithaca, (Ulyses born here.)
7. Cythera, (Venus sprang up here.)
8. Crete, (Minos, lawyer.)
9. Lesbos.
10. Samos.
11. Rhodes.
12. Troy.

IV. POLITICAL HISTORY

1. Heroic Age. (1500 B. C. to 776 B. C.)
 1. Argonautic Expedition—(Golden Fleece.)
 2. The Trojan War.
 3. The Dorian Migration (1104 B. C.)
 4. Homer's Poems { 1. Iliad. 2. Odyssey.
 5. The Amphyctonic Council.

2. Formative Period (776 B. C. to 500 B.C.)
 1. The Olympic Era.
 2. Thirty Tyrants.
 3. Spartan Conquests in the South.
 4. Egypt open to Commerce.
 5. Growth of Athenian Constitution. { 1. Draco. 2. Solon. 3. Pisistratus. 4. Clisthenes.
 6. Growth of Spartan Constitution under the laws of Lycurgus.

3. Persian Wars (500 B. C. to 479 B. C.)
 1. Darius invades Greece. { 1. Marathon. 2. Miltiades. 3. Result.
 2. Preparation of Xerxes—490 B. C. and on.
 3. Second War { 1. Thermopylæ. 2. Salamis. 3. Platea.

4. Athenian Leadership—479 B. C. to 431 B. C.
   1. Age of Pericles.
   2. Athenian Walls.

5. Peloponnesian War (431 B. C. to 404 B. C.)
   1. Persia helps Sparta.
   2. Syracuse (413 B. C.)
   3. Aegospotami (405 B. C.)
   4. The Result.

6. Spartan-Theban Supremacy (404 B. C. to 368 B. C.)
   1. Persian Influence changes.
   2. Peace of Antalcidas 387 B. C.
   3. Cnidus.
   4. Leuctra 371 B. C.
   5. Thebes in Power.

IV. POLITICAL HISTORY.— Con't.

7. Macedonian Supremacy (358 B. C. to 301 B. C.)

1. Philip's Conquests.
   1. In Illyrica.
   2. Aegean Sea.
   3. Part in Sacred War.
   4. Result.
2. The "Philippics" (346 to 340 B. C.)
3. War against Locrians, (340 B. C.)
4. Cheronea, [338 B. C.]
5. Congress at Corinth chooses Alexander.
6. His Conquests.
   1. Granicus, [333 B. C.]
   2. Captures Lydia.
   3. Takes Ephesus.
   4. Issus, [332 B. C.]
   5. Takes
      1. Damascus.
      2. Sidon.
      3. Tyre.
      4. Egypt.
   6. Founds Alexandria.
   7. Takes
      1. Alexandria.
      2. Babylon.
   8. Arbella, (331 B. C.]
   9. Goes to India.
   10. Marriage and Death.
7. The Result.
8. Battle of Ipsus (301 B. C.)

OUTLINES OF GENERAL HISTORY   27

IV. POLITICAL HISTORY —Con't.
  8. Division of Alexander's Kingdom Among his Generals, [323 B. C. to 30 B. C.]
    1. Ptolemy.
      1. Egypt.
      2. Ruled by the family until 30 B. C.
      3. Conquered by Rome.
    2. Cassander.
      1. Macedonia.
      2. Greece.   [B. C.]
        1. Lamnian War, [321
        2. Antipater.
        3. Gauls, 279 B. C.
      3. Taken by Rome [146 B. C.]
    3. Lysimachus.
      1. Thrace and Asia Minor.
      2. Taken by Seleucus, [281 B. C.]
    4. Seleucus.
      1. The East.
      2. India and Syria.
      3. Magnesia, [190 B. C.]
      4. Con. by Rome, [63 B. C.]

V. CIVILIZATION.
  1. Noted because they
    1. Ate at a Public Mess.
    2. Were
      1. Philosophers.
      2. Scientists.
      3. Orators.
      4. Authors.
      5. Inventors.
      6. Discoverers.
      7. Architects.
      8. Warriors.
    3. Had.
      1. Festivals.
      2. Olympic Games.
      3. Gladiatorial Combats.
      4. Theatrical Performances.

28   OUTLINES OF GENERAL HISTORY

V. CIVILI-
ZATION.—
Continued.

{ 4. Invented the Sun-dial.
  5. Made discoveries in Geology and Mathematics.

2. The Schools of Philosophy.
  1. Academic founded by Plato.
  2. Peripatetic founded by Aristotle.
  3. Epicurean, founded by Epicurus.
  4. Stoic, founded by Zeno.

3. Education.
  1. Writing Materials.
    1. The Papyrus.
    2. Parchment.
    3. Wax Tablets.
  2. Libraries become fashionable.
  3. In Athens.
    1. Manners.
    2. Rhythms.
    3. Gymnastics.
    4. *Aesthetic* Education.
  4. In Sparta.
    1. Adroitness.
    2. Skillfulness.
    3. Military Tactics.
    4. *Martial* Education.
  5. Birth of the Drama.

4. Styles of Architecture, and Examples.
  1. Dorian.
    1. Parthenon.
    2. Temple of Zeus, [Jupiter.]
  2. Ionic—Temple of Diana at Ephesus.
  3. Corinthian—Choragic Monument of Lysicrates in Athens.

OUTLINES OF GENERAL HISTORY   29

VI. RELIGION.
1. The 12 Chief Gods and Goddesses.

No.	Greek.	Latin.	Definitions.
1.	Zeus.	Jupiter.	Supreme God.
2.	Hera.	Juno.	Queen of the skies—wife of Jupiter.
3.	Poseidon.	Neptune.	Ruled over the Sea.
4.	Demeter.	Ceres.	Goddess of Agriculture.
5.	Hestia.	Vesta.	Goddess of the Domestic Hearth.
6.	Hephraestus.	Vulcan.	God of Thunder and Fires.
7.	Ares.	Mars.	God of War.
8.	Athena.	Minerva.	Goddess of Wisdom.
9.	Aphrodite	Venus.	Goddess of Love and Beauty.
10.	Apollon.	Apollo.	God of Poetry and Song.
11.	Artemus.	Diana.	Goddess of the chase.
12.	Hermes.	Mercury.	God of Cunning and eloquence.

2. Feast God. { Dionysus. } { Bacchus. } { God of Wine.

3. The Muses.
  1. Clio—History.
  3. Melhomene—Tragedy.
  3. Thalia—Comedy.
  4. Calliope—Epic Poetry.
  5. Urania—Astronomy.
  6. Enterpe—Music.

All daughters of Zeus and Mesonme, (memory) who controlled

3. The Muses. Cont'd.
- 7. Polyhymnia—Oratory.
- 8. Erato—Love Songs.
- 9. Terpsichore—Dancing.

these gifts and met on Mt. Parnassus.

4. The Three Graces of
   - 1. Brightness.
   - 2. Color.
   - 3. Perfume.

5. The Three Fates who spun the Thread of Life.

6. The Three Furies who pursued criminals.

VI. RELIGION. Cont'd.

7. The Three Hesperides, daughters of Atlas, in whose garden the golden apples grew, and who held the world on his back.

8. Nature of
   - 1. They worshiped all these gods, &c., and others.
   - 2. Believed in oracles, prophecies and dreams.
   - 3. General character—Mythological.

No.	Centuries B.C	Name.	Where born?	Cause of Fame, &c.
1	8th	Hesiod	Boetia	A Poet.
2	7th	Anaximander	Sardis	Poet. Invents Sun-dial.
3		Periander	Corinth	A Tyrant.
4	6th	Pythagoras	Samos	Traveller and Mathematician.
5		Sappho	Lesbos	Poetess.
6		Solon	Athens	Lawyer and Poet.
7		Thales	Miletus	Astronomer and Philosopher.
8	5th	Aeschylus	Athens	Author, (60 Tragedies.)
9		Aeschines	same	Orator.
10		Plato	same	Teacher—Dialogues.
11		Socrates	same	Teacher— Philosopher.
12	4th	Aristides	same	General and Party Leader.
13		Aristophanes	same	Author, (40 Comedies.)
14		Demosthenes	same	Orator—("Philippics.")
15		Euripides	same	Author. (75 ragedies.)
16		Epaminondas	Thebes	General.
17		Herodotus	Asia Minor	Historian-"Father of History."
18		Pericles	Athens	Orator and General. [thenon.
19		Phidias	same	Architect—Designs the Par-
20		Sophocles	same	Author. (70 Tragedies.)
21		Themistocles	same	General—Hero of Athenians.
22		Thucydides	same	Historian.
23		Xenophon	same	Historian and General.
24		Diogenes	inope	Philosopher.
25		Epicurus	Samos	Teacher and Philosopher.
26	3rd	Hippocrates	Corinth	Physician.
27		Archimedes	Syracuse	inventor and Philosopher.
28		Euclid		Teacher at Alexandria.
29		Epicurus	Samos	Teacher and Philosopher.
30		Aristotle	Macedonia	Peacher and Philosopher, taught Alexander the Great.
31		Theocritus	Syracuse	Poet.
32		Georgias	Sicily	Orator.

33. For others. see outline on Political History.

Chapter X.—(8) Rome.

I. GEOGRAPHICAL DIVISIONS.
- 1. Northern Italy.
  - 1. Istria.
  - 2. Venetia.
  - 3. Cisalpine Gaul.
  - 4. Liguria.
  - 5. Etruria.
- 2. Central Italy.
  - 1. Umbria.
  - 2. Sabini.
  - 3. Picenum.
  - 4. Latium.
  - 5. Vestini.
  - 6. Campania.
  - 7. Samnium.
- 3. Southern Italy.
  - 1. Apulia.
  - 2. Lapygia.
  - 3. Lucania.
  - 4. Bruttium.

II. LOCATION AND SIZE.
1. A Peninsula in Southern Europe.
2. It is 2700 miles long and 1000 miles, average breath.

III. COUNTRIES AT GREATEST EXTENT.

1. Spain.
2. Portugal.
3. France.
4. Belgium.
5. Holland.
6. Russia (part of)
7. Bavaria.
8. Switzerland.
9. Italy.
10. Austria.
11. Hungary.
12. Russia (part of)
13. Servia.
14. Turkey.
15. Greece.
16. Asia Minor.
17. Syria.
18. Palestine.
19. Egypt.
20. Tripoli.
21. Tunis.
22. Algeria.
23. Morocco.
24. Idumea.
25. Britanny.

27. Provinces for Government.

OUTLINES OF GENERAL HISTORY 33

III. POLITICAL HISTORY.
- 1. The First Empire, (753 B. C. to 509 B. C.)
  - 1. Early Races.
    - 1. Etruscans.
    - 2. Italians.
      - 1. Latins.
      - 2. Umbro-Sabellians.
        - 1. Umbr-ans.
        - 2. Oscans.
        - 3. Sabeins.
        - 4. Samnites.
        - 5. Sabellians.
  - 2. Location of Rome, (city.)
  - 3. The Seven Kings.
  - 4. Servian Constitution.
  - 5. Patricians and Plebeians.
  - 6. Etruscan Conquest.
  - 2. Location of Rome.
    - 1. On the Seven Hills.
      - 1. Aventine.
      - 2. Capitoline.
      - 3. Aesquiline.
      - 4. Palatine.
      - 5. Caelian.
      - 6. Viminal.
      - 7. Quirinal.
    - 2. The Fable
  - 3. Kings
    - 1. The Seven Kings
      - 1. Romulus.
      - 2. Numa Hostilius.
      - 3. Tullius.
      - 4. Ancus Martius.
      - 5. Tarquin the Elder.
      - 6. Servius Tullius.
    - 2. Stories.
  - 4. Servian Constitution.
  - 5. Patricians and Plebeians.
  - 6. Etruscan Conquest.

III. POLITICAL HISTORY. Cont'd.	2. The Republic, (509 B. C. to 30 B. C.)	1. Wars for Existence, (509 B. C. to 343 B. C.)	1. The first consuls. 2. Secession of Plebians. 3. Tribunes and Censors. 4. Patriots and Heroes. {1. Coriolanus. 2. Cincinnatus. 3. Horatius.} 5. The Decemvirs, (451 B. C.) 6. The Gauls in Rome, (390 B. C.)
		2. Wars for Foreign Possession of Italy, (343 to 264 B. C.)	1. First Samnite War, (343 to 341 B. C.) 2. Great Latin War, (340 to 338 B. C.) 3. Second Samnite War, (326 to 304 B. C.) 4. Third Samnite War, (208 to 290 B. C.) 5. "Pyrrhic War," (280 to 276 B. C.) {1. Heraclea 2. Beneventum.}
		3. Wars for Foreign Dominion. (264 B.C. to 133 B. C.)	1. The first Punic War, (294 to 241 B. C.) 2. The Second Punic War, (218 to 201 B. C.) {1. Tiebia—218 B. C. 2. Trasimenus—217 B. C. 3. Caunae—216 B. C. 4. Size of Capua. 5. Metaurus—207 B. C. 6. Zama—202 B. C. 7. Hannibal. 8. Scipio.}

III. Political History —Con'td.
2. The Republic, (509 B. C. to 30 B. C.) Cont'd.

3. Wars for Foreign Dominion, (264 to 133 B. C.)
  3. Second Macedonian War—200 to 197 B. C.
  4. Battle of Magnesia—190 B. C.
  5. The Macedonian War (171 to 168 B. C.)
     I. Pydna—168 B. C.
     2. Result.
  6. The Third Punic War, (149 to 146 B. C.
     1. Fall of Carthage—146 B. C.
     2. Fall of Corinth—146 B. C.
     3. Results.
  7. Tiberius Gracchus.

4. Civil Wars, (133 B. C. to 30 B. C.)
  1. Servile war in Sicily—133 to 132 B. C.
  2. Public Lands.
  3. Reforms of the Gracchi.
     1. Tiberius.
     2. Caius.
  4. War with Jugurtha—111 to 106 B. C.
  5. Cimbri and Teutonic Invasion—101 B. C.
  6. Social War—91 to 89 B. C.
     1. Marius.
     2. Sulla.
  7. First Mithridactic War.
  8. Pompey in Spain.
  9. War of Gladiators.
  10. War with Mediterranean Pirates—66 B. C.
  11. Second Mithridactic War—66 to 63 B. C.
  12. Cataline's Conspiracy.

36 OUTLINES OF GENERAL HISTORY

III. POLITICAL HISTORY. Cont'd.
- 2. The Republic, (509 B. C. to 30 B. C.) Cont'd.
  - 4. Civil Wars, (133 B. C. to 30 B. C.)
    - 13. First Triumviate—60 B. C.
      - 1. Men
        - 1. Cæsar
        - 2. Pompey.
        - 3. Crassus.
      - 2. Pharsalus.
      - 3. Result.
    - 14. Second Triumviate—43 B. C.
      - 1. Men
        - 1. Augustus.
        - 2. Antony.
        - 3. Lepidus.
      - 2. Philippi.
      - 3. Actium—31 B. C.
      - 4. Results.
- 3. The Second Empire—30 B. C. to 476 A. D.
  - 1. Reign of Augustus—30 B. C. to 14 A. D.
    - 1. Extent of his Kingdom.
    - 2. Defeat of Varus—9 A. D.
    - 3. His Public Works.
    - 4. BIRTH OF CHRIST.
  - 2. Reign of Tiberius—14 to 37 A. D.
    - 1. Death of Christ.
    - 2. Other Events.
  - 3. Reign of Caligula—37 to 41 A. D.
  - 4. Claudius—41 to 54 A. D.
  - 5. Nero—54 to 68 A. D.
    - 1. Great Fire.
    - 2. Cruelty.
  - 6. Galba, Otho, Vitella—68 to 69 A. D.

III. POLITICAL HISTORY. Cont'd.
- 3. The Second Empire —30 B. C. to 476 A. D. Cont'd.
  - 7. Vespasian. —69 79.
    - 1. Jesusalem captured.
    - 2. Eruption of Vesuvius.
  - 8. Titus—79 to 81 A. D.
  - 9. Domitian—81 to 06 A. D.
  - 10. The Good Emperors —96 to 180 A. D.
    - 1. Nerva.
    - 2. Trajan.
    - 3. Hadrian.
    - 4. Autonius Pius.
    - 5. Autonius—Marcus Aurelius.
  - 11. Commodus—180 to 192 A. D.
  - 12. The Barrack Emperors— 192 to 284 A. D.
    - 1. Public Sale of Empire.
    - 2. Septimus Serverus.
    - 3. Caracalla.
    - 4. Alexander Scrverus.
    - 5. Thirty Tyrants— 251 to 258 A. D.
    - 6. Fall of Palmyra.
    - 7. Illyrian Emperors— 268 to 284 A. D.
      - 1. Claudius.
      - 2. Aurelius.
      - 3. Probus.
      - 4. Diocletian.
      - 5. Maximian.
  - 13. Diocletian—284 to 305 A. D.
  - 14. Constantine— 305 to 337 A. D.
    - 1. Nicene Creed—325 A. D.
    - 2. Constantinople.
    - 3. State Religion.
    - 4. Absolutism.

III. POLITICAL HISTORY. Continued.
{
  3. The Second Empire—30 B. C. to 476 A. D. Cont'd.
  {
    15. Julian. the Apostate—361 to 363 A. D.

    16. Valentinian and Valens— 363 to 379 A. D. { 1. Barbarians. 2. Goths. }

    17. Theodo- sius the Great— 379 to 395 A. D. { 1. Division of Empire. 2. Last Triumph. 3. Gladiatorial Combats. }

    18. Honorius { 1. Alaric. 2. The Ransom. 3. Stilicho. 4. Western Empire seized. 5. Eastern Empire. }

    19. The Barbarians. {
      1. The Huns. { 1. Attila. 2. Chalons— 451 A. D. }
      2. The Vandals. { 1. Genseric. 2. Vandalism. }
      3. Its Downfall— 476 B. C. { 1. Romulus Augustulus 2. Zeno, Emp. of East. 3. Odoacer, Patrician. }
    }
  }
}

IV. CIVILIZATION.
1. Kinds of Civilization.
   1. Latin.
   2. Greek.
   3. Oriental.
2. Population at its greatest extent, 1,000,000,000 people.
3. Rome had
   1. 20 miles of Walls pierced with 30 Gates.
   2. The Colisseum.
   3. The Capitol.
   4. Circus Maximus.
   5. The Forum.
4. Temple of Janus.
5. The People are noted for their
   1. Aqueducts.
   2. Baths.
   3. Cruel Kings.
   4. Orators.
   5. Generals.
   6. Slaves.
   7. Dress and Food.
6. Literature.
   1. They wrote with the stylus on parchment and skins.
   2. Authors and noted books
      1. Virgil—"Aenid"
      2. Sallust—"Jugurthine War."
      3. Cæsar—"Commentaries."
      4. Horace—Poet.
      5. Livy.
      6. Pliny.
      7. Tacitus.
      8. Catullus.
      9. Cicero.
7. Religion, (See Greece.)
8. They copied and borrowed many customs from Greece and elsewhere.

VI.—GREAT MEN.

No.	Dates.	Names.	Birth and Circumstances.	Cause of Fame.
1	B. C. 3d Century	Regulus..........	Rome—Patrician.	Consul and General.
2		Scipio Africanus......	Rome—Pat.........	Victor of Zama (201 B. C.)
3		Marcellus....	Rome—Plebeian..	Gen. Conquered Syracuse
4		Fabius Maximus............	Rome—Patrician.	Consul—"Delayer of Hannibal."
5	2d cent.	Ennius..........	Apulia—Free......	Translator of Greek Dramas.
6		Andronicus..	Tarentum—Slave	Presented the first Drama.
7		Cato, the Elder...........	Rome—Plebeian..	Censor, Orator and Author.
8		Planutus.......	Umbria—Free......	Wrote 21 Latin Comedies
9		Polybius.......	Greece—Free.......	"Universial History."
10		Scipio, the Younger.....	Rome—Patrician.	Conquers Carthage and Spain.
11		Terence.........	Carthage—Slave.	Author—Latin Comedies
12	1st cent.	Cato, the Younger..	Utica—Plebeian..	Orator and General under Pompey.
13	A. D. 1st Century	Agrippa..........	Rome—Latin.......	General and Surveyor.
14		Diodorus.....	Sicily—Greek......	"General History."
15		Dionysius......	Assyria—Greek...	History and Rhetoric.
16		Epictetus......	Phrygia—Slave...	Philosopher.
17		Horace...........	Apulia—Free......	Latin Satires and Poems
18		Josephus........	A Greek Jew.......	Historian of Judea.
19		Livy.............	Padua—Latin......	"History of Rome."
20		Ovid..............	Italy—Latin........	Poet- "Metamorphoses."
21		Quintillian....	Spain—Latin......	Lawyer, Orator and Rhetorician.
22		Pliny, the Elder,.............	Gaul—Latin........	Wrote on Natural Science
23		Seneca,...........	Spain—Latin.....	Philosophical Author.
24		Virgil............	Mantua—Free.....	Poet—"The Aeneid."
25		Vitrurius....	Verona—Free......	Architect—Inspector for Augustus.

VI.—GREAT MEN.—Continued.

No.	Dates.	Names.	Birth and Circumstances.	Cause of Fame.
26	2d cent.	Apuleius	Africa—Slave	Author—"Golden Ass."
27		Arrian	Asia—Greek	Author—"Alexander and His Successors."
28		Galen	Pergamos—Greek	Physician of M. Aurelius
29		Justin Martyr	Samaria—Greek	Philosopher.
30		Juvenal	Italy—Free	Latin Satirical Poems.
31	A. D. 2d Century	Plutarch	Boetia—Greek	Biographical Author.
32		Ptolmey	Egypt—Greek	Mathematician—"Almagest."
33		Pliny, the Younger	Gaul—Latin	Lawyer—Descriptive Letters.
34		Tacitus	Italy—Latin	Historian—"Germania"
35	3d cent.	St. Clement	Alexandria—Greek	Author—Christian Doctrine.
36		St. Cyprian	Carthage—Latin	Father of the Poor.
37		Origen	Alexandria—Greek	Author—Theology and Literature.
38		Porphyry	Syria—Greek	Opposed Christianity.
39		Tertullian	Carthage—Latin	An Ascetic, Argued against Paganism.
40		Ulpian	Tyre—Latin	Lawyer and Author.
41	4th cent.	St. Ambrose	Gaul—Latin	Commentaries and Sermons.
42		St. Anthony	Egypt—Latin	Author and Lawyer—Father of Monasticism.
42		Arius	Egypt—Greek	Author—Establishes Arian Heresy.
43		Athanasius	Egypt—Greek	Author—Defends Orthodoxy.
43		St. Augustine	Numidia—Latin	Bishop—Theology and Rhetoric.
44		Constantine	Moesia—Latin	Emp. Founder of Constantinople.
45		St. Basil	Cappadocia—Greek	Teacher and Founder of Houses of Refuge and Orphanages.

VI.—GREAT MEN.—Continued.

No.	Dates.	Names.	Birth and Circumstances.	Cause of Fame.
46		St. Chrysostom......	Antioch—Greek...	Preacher and Author—Commentaries.
47		St. Jerome.....	—Latin......	Translates the Bible into Latin.
47		Julian...........	Greece—Greek Nephew of Constantine............	Emperor and Author—Attacks Christianity.
48		Theodosius....	Son of Julian—Latin..............	Emp. and Lawyer—"Theodosian Code."
49		Ulfilas............	A Goth...............	Missionary—Translates Bible into Gothic.
50	5th cent.	Alaric. ⎫ Barbarians.	A Visigoth...........	King and General.
51		Attila. ⎬	A Hun................	Leader and General.
52		Genseric. ⎭	A Vandal...........	General from Africa.
53		Leo I.............	Rome—Latin.......	Pope and Author—Sermons, &c.
54		Odoacer.........	A Teuton.............	"Patrician of Italy."
55		Stilicho..........	Rome—Latin.......	General.
56		St. Patric......	Rome—Latin.......	Author Roman Alphabet
57		Zosimus.........	Rome—Latin.......	Historian and Lawyer.

See outline of Literature for others.

Chapter XI.—Mediaeval History.

I. DATES.
- 1. Dark Ages—from 476 A. D. to 1100 A. D.
- 2. Dawn—from 1100 A. D. to 1500 A. D.

II. THE TEUTONS.
- 1. Divisions.
  - 1. Ostrogoths—493-554.
    - 1. Odoacer.
    - 2. Theodoric.
  - 2. Visigoths—415-711—Roderic.
  - 3. The Burgundians—443-534.
  - 4. The Vandals—429-533.
    - 1. Genseric.
    - 2. In Italy.
    - 3. Defeated by Belisarius.
  - 5. Merovingians—486 to 752—Clovis
  - 6. Lombards—568 to 774.
  - 7. Anglo-Saxons in Britain—827.
  - 8. Northmen.
    - 1. In France.
    - 2. In England.
    - 3. In Russia.
    - 4. In Iceland.
- 2. Conversion to Christianity.
- 3. Formation of Romance Languages.

III. BYZANTIUM.
- 1. Reign of Justinian 527-565.
  - 1. Roman Law.
  - 2. Trebonian.
- 2. Reign of Heraclius—610-641.
  - 1. His Character.
  - 2. Battle of Nineveh.
- 3. Estern Empire passes to the Greeks.
- 4. Downfall of Constantinople—1453.

IV. MOHAMMEDANISM AND THE SARACENS.
- 1. Birth of Mohammed—571.
- 2. The Hegira—622.
- 3. The Religion.
  - 1. Doctrines.
  - 2. The "Koran."
- 4. Death of Mohammed—632.
- 5. Conquests of the Saracens.
- 6. Battle of Tours—732.
  - 1. Chas Martel.
  - 2. Loss of Men—375,000.
- 7. The Ottoman Empire.
- 8. Saracen Divisions.

V. Charlemagne.
1. His Birth—742.
2. Becomes King—768.
3. Organizes Holy Roman Empire—800.
4. His Death—814.
5. His Works.
6. His Kingdom.
   1. Treaty of Verdun—843.
   2. Division.

VI. The Crusades.

1. Greater Crusades.

No.	Dates.	Leaders.	Objects.	Results.
1	1096 to 1099.	Peter, the Hermit. Walter the Penniless. Godfrey of Bouillon. Duke of Lorraine.	Rescue the Holy Sepulcher.	Captured Antioch, Nice and Jerusalem. A Latin Kingdom.
2	1147 to 1149.	St. Bernard. Conrad III, Louis VII.	Defend the Sacred Place.	Defeated in Asia Minor.
3	1189 to 1192.	Frederick Barbarossa. Philip Augustus. Richard I.	Recovery of Jerusalem from Saladin.	Captured Acre. The "Truce."
4	1202 to 1204.	Alexius.	Directed against Constantinople.	Its capture. Twice held, but re-captured in 1261 by Greeks.

2. Children's Crusade and Results.
3. Lesser Crusades.

5	1216 to 1220.	Kings of Hungary and Cyprus.	To Conquer Egypt.	Nothing.
6	1227 to 1229.	Frederick II.	Same as 2nd Crusade.	Secured restoration of Jerusalem.
7	1249 to 1254.	St. Louis IX.	Set up a Kingdom in Africa.	Nothing. Louis dies in Egypt.
8	1270 to 1272.	Louis IX. Edward I.	Africa and Palestine.	Edward captures Nazareth. A Treaty.

VII. THE HUNDRED YEARS WAR. (1336-1453.)
1. Cause—Lands of England in France.
2. Events
   1. Battle of Crecy—1346.
   2. Capture of Calais by the English
   3. Battle of Poitiers—1356.
      1. Edward VI.
      2. French.
         1. John.
         2. Philip.
      3. Result.
   4. Battle of Agincourt—1415.
   5. Siege of Orleans—1429.
      1. Joan of Arc.
      2. The Dauphin Crowned
   6. Joan of Arc burned—1431.
   7. English Reverses.
   8. Treaties
      1. Bretigny—1360.
      2. Troyes—1419.
      3. Arras—1435.
3. Summary.

VIII. WAR OF THE ROSES—1455-1485
1. Cause
   1. Dispute as to the Title to the Crown by the Houses of York and Lancaster.
   2. Why so called?
2. Events.
   1. Battle of St. Albans—1455.
   2. Battle of Blore Heath—1459.
   3. Wakefield and Towton—1461.
   4. Hexham—1464.
   5. Barnet—1471.
   6. Bosworth Field—1485.
   7. Warwick, the King maker.
3. Summary.
   1. Cost England
      1. 12 Princes.
      2. 200 Nobles.
      3. 100,000 people.
      4. Much money.
   2. Result. House of Lancaster Regains the Throne.

IX. RISE OF MODERN NATIONS.
1. France.
2. Spain.
3. Italy.
4. Russia.
5. Germany
6. England.

1. FRANCE
—987 to
1498.

   1. Capetian Period
—987
1328.

      1. Acquisition of English Territory—1066.
      2. Holy Wars for Recovery of Jerusalem.
      3. Crusades against Albigenses—1202—1229.
      4. Creation of States General—1302.
      5. Triumph of Absolutism.
      6. Rulers of this Period
          1. Philip Augustus
          2. Louis IX.
          3. Philip IV.
          4. Louis XI.

   2. House of Valois—1328—1498.

      1. Hundred Years War with England—1328—1453.
      2. Trouble with Charles the Bold of Burgundy 1461—1483.
      3. Charles VIII. invades Italy—1490.
      4. His retreat back to Paris.
      5. Feudal System at an end.

2. SPAIN—
732 to
1516.

   1. The Moors in Spain.
      1. Their Kingdom.
      2. Cordova.
   2. Queen Isabella of Castile marries Ferdinand of Aragon—1469.
   3. Union of the Colonies—1479.
   4. Expulsion of the Moors—1480—1491.
   5. Discovery of America—1492.
   6. Death of the Sovereigns.
      1. Isabella—1504.
      2. Ferdinand—1516.
   7. The Inquisition.

IX. RISE OF MODERN NATIONS. Cont'd.

3. ITALY 843 to 1499
1. No Government since 843.
2. See No. 3 in outline of Germany.
3. Rienzi's stand for Liberty—1347.
4. The Renaissance.
5. Savonarola—1452—1498.
6. The City Republics.
   1. Florence.
   2. Venice.
   3. Genoa.
   4. Naples.

4. RUSSIA—837—1505.
1. Ruric the Red, 837. Its Rise
2. Conquest of Tartars in the 13th century.
3. Freedom under Ivan the Great, 1462-1505.
4. Her Boundaries.

5. Germany—843—1519.
1. Carolingians—843—911.
   1. Lothair.
   2. Otto the Great.
2. Conrad of Franconia—911-919.
3. Saxon Emperors 919—1024
   1. Renewal of the Empire—962.
   2. Guelphs and Ghibellines.
4. Lothair of Saxony—1125—1137.
5. Hohenstaufen Family—1137—1254.
   1. Frederick Barbarossa.
   2. Cathedral Building—1248.
6. Interregnum & Different Emp.—1254—1273 to 1438.
   1. Rise of the Swiss Republic, 1315, 1388
      1. Morgarten
      2. Sempach.
      3. Nafels.
   2. Rise of Austria.
   3. Character of her rulers.
7. House of Hapsburg.
   1. Albert, Duke Austria, 1438-1493
   2. Maximilian I.—1493—1519.
   3. The Hussites.

48   OUTLINES OF GENERAL HISTORY

IX. RISE OF
MODERN
NATIONS.
Cont'd.

6. England.
(827–1499.)

1. Roman Conquest.

2. Saxon Dynasty—827–1016.
  1. Rulers.
    1. Egbert—827.
    2. Ethelbert.
    3. Alfred the Great—871–901.
    4. Edward the Elder—901-925
    5. Athelstane—925–941.
    6. The six Boy Kings—941-1016.
  2. The Danish Conquest—1016.

3. Danish and Restored Saxon Dynasty—1016 to 1066.
  1. Rulers.
    1. Canute—1016-1035.
    2. Harold Harefoot—1035-1040
    3. Hardicanute.—1040-1042.
    4. Edward the Confessor—1042-1066
    5. Harold. II—1066.
  2. Battle of Hastings—1066.
  3. Norman Conquest.

4. The Normans—1066-1154.
  1. Rulers.
    1. William I. 1066-1087
    2. William II. 1087-1100. a
    3. Henry I. 1100-1135. b
    4. Matilda and Stephen—1135-1154.
  2. Their Character.
    a. Called Rufus, the red-haired.
    b. Fine Scholar.

OUTLINES OF GENERAL HISTORY 49

IX. RISE OF MODERN NATIONS.—Cont'd.

6. England—827—1499.—Continued.

5. The Plantagenets.

1. Rulers.
1. Henry II—1154-1189.
2. Richard I—1189-1199.
3. John—1199-1216.
4. Henry III—1216-1272.
5. Edward I—1272-1307.
6. Edward II—1307-1327.
7. Edward III—1327-1377.
8. Richard II—1377-1399.
9. Henry IV—1399-1413
10. Henry V—1413-1422. } House of York.
11. Henry VI—1422-1461.
12. Edward IV—1461-1483
13. Edward V—one year. } House of Lancaster
14. Richard III—1483-1485
a15. Henry VII—See modern outline.

2. Events.
1. Growth of Liberty.
  1. John's Trouble.
  2. Magna Charta—1216.
  3. House of Commons 14th century.
  4. Earl Simon de Montfort.
2. Conquest of Ireland under Henry II.
3. Conquest of Wales by Edward I.
4. Conquest of Scotland by Edward III.
  1. Wallace
  2. Bruce.
  3. Effect.

a. Founder of the House of Tudors.

OUTLINES OF GENERAL HISTORY

IX. RISE OF MODERN NATIONS.—Cont'd.
- 6. England (827-1499)—Continued.
  - 5. The Plantagenets. Con'd.
    - c. Events.—Cont'd.
      - 5. Hundred Years War, (see p. 45.)
      - 6. War of the Roses, (see p. 45.)
      - 7. Founding of the Tudor Line of Sovereigns.
      - 8. Discoveries and Explorations.
        - 1. The Cabots, (1497)
        - 2. Drake, (1569-1579.)

X. CIVILIZATION.
- 1. Religion.
  - 1. Forms.
    - 1. Roman Catholic.
    - 2. Greek.
    - 3. Others
      - 1. Albigenses.
      - 2. Huguenots, etc.
  - 2. Characteristic features of each.
- 2. Literature.
  - 1. In France.
    - 1. Troubadours and Trouveurs.
    - 2. Froissart's Chronicle—1337-1410. ["Cid."
  - 2. In Spain—Romances of the
  - 3. In Germany.
    - 1. The "Neibelunzelied"
    - 2. The Minnesingers.
  - 4. In England. 1328-1400
    - 1. Chaucer—
      - 1. Father of Poetry.
      - 2. Canterbury Tales.
    - 2. Wycliffe translates the Bible—1380.
- 3. Art.
  - 1. Leonardo Vinci—1415-1459.
  - 2. Michael Angelo, Artist—1472-1564.
  - 3. Raphael—1483-1520.
  - 4. Titian—1477-1576.

  All in Italy.

X. CIVILI-
ZATION.—
Cont'd.
- 4. Monasticism.
- 5. Rise of Papacy.
- 6. Feudalism.
- 7. Chivalry.
  - 1. Page.
  - 2. Squire.
  - 3. Knight.
- 8. The Tournament.

X. CIVILI-
ZATION.—
Cont'd.
- 9. Noted for
  - 1. Relapse into Ignorance.
  - 2. Extravagance in dress.
  - 3. Royal Entertainments.
  - 4. Serving Foreign Delicacies.
  - 5. Costly Tableware, but had no knives and forks.
  - 6. Severely punishing for mild offenses.
- 10. Inventions.
  - 1. Roger Bacon makes known the use of Gunpowder.
  - 2. Gutenburg invents printing in 1456.
  - 3. Caxton's typographic printing in England at Westminster—1460-1491.
  - 4. General effect on history.

XI.—GREAT MEN.

No.	Century	Names.	Chief Work.	Character or Profession.	Language.
1	6th	St. Augustine	Founder of Order of Monks.	Author and teacher.	Latin.
2		Belisarius	Fought the Barbarians.	General of Justinian	
3		St. Benedict	Founded an Order of Monks.	Preacher and Author	Latin.
4		Boethius	Theology and Philosophy.	Translator.	Latin.
5		Clovius	King of the Franks.	Ruler	Latin and Gothic.
6		Justinian	Emp. of Byzantium.	Ruler	Latin.
7		Theodoric	Emp. Western Empire.	Ruler	Latin and Gothic.
8		Trebonian	Codes, Pandects and Institutes.	Law-giver of Justinian	
9	7th	Caedmon	Paraphrase of Scriptures.	Poet.	Latin. English.
10		Mohammed	Founds a new religion.	Preacher and teacher	Arabic.
11		Omar	Translates into Greek, Latin and English.	Preacher and Ruler.	Arabic.
12	8th	Alcuin	Philosophy and Theology.	Author and Scholar.	Latin.
13		"The Venerable" Bede.	Translation of Bible	Historian and author	Latin and English.
14		Charlemagne.	King of the Franks.	General and Ruler.	Latin and French.
15		Charles Martel	Stopped Mohammedans.	General	French (?)
16		Dungal	Lectured in Paris.	Teacher	Latin.
17		Cynewulf	"Wife's Complaint"	Poet.	English.
18		Haroun-al-Raschid	Mohammedan Ruler	Author.	Arabic.
19		Geber	Translations.	Chemist and Doctor	Arabic and English.
20	9th	Alfred the Great	King of England.	Author, Historian, &c.	English.
21		Al Mamun	A Mohammedan Author.	Translator.	Arabic.
22		Asser	Philosophy, etc.	Author	Ara. & Lat.

No.	Century	Names.	Chief Work.	Character or Profession.	Language.
23	10th	Hugh Capet	Founder of French Monarchy	King	French.
24		Otto I	Conqueror of Germany	King	German.
25		Rollo	Conquers Normandy	General and King	Norse, French
26	11th	Albucasis	Anatomy and Physics	Translator.	Arabic and Latin.
27		Anselm	Scholastic Works	Author	Latin.
28		Hildebrand	Becomes Pope	Spiritual Teacher	Latin.
29		William I	Conqueror of England	General and King	Norman and French.
30		Peter the Hermit	Preached the Crusades	Preacher and Monk	Latin.
31	12th	Abelard	Taught at Paris-Heretic	Teacher and Author	Latin.
32		Aber Ezra	Work on Scriptures	Author and Translator.	Hebrew.
33		Averroes (of Cordova)	Languages and Mathematics.	Author	Arabic.
34		Thomas, a Becket	Disagreement with Henry II., Chancellor of England.	Author	English and Latin.
35		Frederick Barbarasa	Of Germany.	Great Crusader and Ruler	German.
36		Godfrey of Bouillon	France and England		French.
37		Richard I.			English.
38		Saladin	Founds Mohammedan Dynasty	Ruler and General	Arabic.
39	13th	Albertus Magnus	Natural Science	Author and Teacher	Latin.
40		Alfonso, the Wise	Translates Bible into Spanish	Author	Latin and Spanish.
41		Roger Bacon.	Invents Telescope and Gunpowder, &c.	Inventor	Latin.

No.	Century	Names.	Chief Works.	Character or Profession.	Language.
42		Edward I, (of Eng.)	Eng. Laws. History of Chronicles—Wales Constitution	Ruler and Author	English.
43		Stephen Langton	"Magna Charta"	Author	English.
44		St. Louis	French Law from Roman	Ruler and Author	French.
45		Peter de Crescenzi	Botany	Author	English and Italian.
46		Marco Polo	Book of Travels	Traveler	French and Italian.
47	14th	Boccaccio	"Decameron"	Author	Italian.
48		Robert Bruce	Scottish Warrior	General	Scotch.
49		Chaucer	"Canterbury tales"	Poet	English.
50		Dante, (Alighieri)	"Inferno"	Author	Italian.
51		Froissart	Chronicles of Eng. and French History	Historian	French.
52		Giotto	Author of Bell Tower at Florence	Architect	Italian.
53		Sir Jno. Mandeville	Book of Travels	Author	Latin. Eng. French.
54		Rienzi (Coladi.)	Last of the Tribunes	Leader and Patriot	Italian.
55		Wat Tyler	Opposed Absolutism	General	English.
56		Sir Wm. Wallace	Scotch Patriot	Author and General	English.
57		John Wycliffe	Translates Bible	Author	English.
58	15th	Pius II	Mathematics	Pope and Author	Latin.
59		Buenelschi	Author of the Dome of Rome	Architect	Latin.
60		Wm. Caxton	First Printing in England	Inventor & Printer	English.

No.	Century	Names.	Chief Work.	Character or Profession	Language.
61	15th	Cusamus	Law and Theories Fore-runner of Copernicus	Lawyer and Astronomer	Latin.
62		Donatello	"Judith holding the Head of Holoferness	Carver and Sculptor	Latin.
63		Gutenburg	Printing by Movable Types	Inventor & Printer	German.
64		John Huss	Followers of Wycliffe	Authors and Reformers	Latin and Bohemian.
65		Jerome of Prague			
66		Joan of Arc	The Peasant Girl who led French Armies	Leader	French.
67		*Savonarola	Catholic Reformer	Monk and Author	Italian.
68		*Van Enycks	Originator of Painting in Oils	Great Painter	Italian.
69		*Lorenzo de Medici	Founds Schools and Libraries	Statesman and Patron of Arts	Latin.
70		*Columbus	Discovers America	Explorer & Navigator	Spanish.
71		*John Cabot	Discovers N. A.	Sailor	English.
72		*Waldsee Muller	Names America in Honor of Vespucci (Amerigo.)	Geographer	German.

*All Born in Italy.

Chapter XII.—Modern History.

I. Events of the 16th Century.
  1. The French in Italy.
     1. Rulers
        1. Charles VIII.—1483-1498.
        2. Louis XI.—1498-1515.
        3. Francis I.—1515-1547.
     2. Object of Invasions.
     3. Battles.
        1. Fornovo.
        2. Naples.
        3. Venice.
        4. Milan.
        5. Of the Spurs.
        6. Marignano.
     4. Leagues.
        1. First League.
        2. League of Cambray.
        3. Holy League.
        4. League of Malines.
     5. Results.
  2. Charles V. and Reformation.
  3. Rise of the Dutch Republic.
  4. Civil and Religious War of France.
  5. England under the Tudors.

II. Events on the 17th Century.
  1. The Thirty Years War.
  2. Monarchy in France.
  3. England under the Stuarts.

III. Events of the 18th Century.
  1. Peter the Great and Charles XII.
  2. Rise of Prussia.
  3. England under Hanover, (House of Brunswick.
  4. The French Revolution.

IV. Events of the 19th Century.
  1. French Revolution and France.
  2. England under House of Brunswick.
  3. Other Modern Nations.

V. Great Men of Centuries.

Chapter XIII.—The Reformation.

(2) CHARLES V. AND THE REFORMATION—1517-60.
- 1. Genealogy.
  1. Son of Philip, the Handsome.
  2. Grandson of Maximilian I. and Ferdinand and Isabella.
- 2. His Rivals.
  1. Francis I. of France.
  2. Henry VIII. of England.
  3. Solyman, the Magnificent of Turkey.
- 3. Luther.—1483-1546.
  1. His Theses.
  2. Edict of the Pope.
  3. Diet of Worms—1521.
- 4. The First Protestants—1529.
- 5. Diets of
  1. Spires.
  2. Augsburg.
- 6. The first War against Francis—1521-26.
  1. Battle of Pavia—1525.
  2. Treaty of Madrid.
- 7. Second War against Francis—1527-29.
  1. Imperial army in Rome.
  2. Ladies' Peace—1529.
- 8. Third War against Francis—1536-28.
  1. Solyman aids Francis.
  2. Turks in Hungary and Tunis.
  3. Treaty of Nice--1538.
- 9. Fourth War—1542-44.
  1. Treaty of Crespy—1544.
  2. Results.
- 10. His Protestant Wars—1531-60.
  1. Smalcaldic League—1531.
  2. Charles' Triumph—1547.
  3. Revolt of Maurice.
  4. Treaty of Passau—1552.
  5. His abdication of the throne—1556.
  6. St. Quentin—1557.
  7. Treaty of Cateau-Cambresis—1559.
- 11. His character.

Chapter XIV.—Dutch Republic.

(3) RISE OF THE DUTCH REPUBLIC—1568-1609.

3. War for Freedom—1568-1609.

1. Position of the Netherlands.
   1. On the North Sea.
   2. As large as Ohio. (?)*
2. Queen Margaret's Persecutions of the Heretics.
3. Dutch.
   1. Leaders.
      1. Spanish.
         1. Don John.
         2. Duke of Alva.
         3. Requesens.
         4. Valdez.
         5. Duke of Parma.
      2. Dutch.
         1. Egmond.
         2. Horn.
         3. Maurice of Nassau.
         4. Sir Philip Sidney.
         5. William the Silent.
   2. Events.
      1. Pacification of Ghent—1577.
      2. Jealousy of the sections.
      3. Union of Utrecht—1579.
      4. The Ban and Apology.
      5. Assassination of William—1584.
      6. England aids the Dutch.
      7. Treaty of 1609.
4. Its Development.
   1. The Fields like Gardens.
   2. Afterwards aids England.
   3. Advanced as Spain declined.
   4. Their Industry and Intelligence.

Chapter XV.—Wars of France.

(4) CIVIL AND RELIGIOUS WARS OF FRANCE—1562-1610

1. Persecution of the Huguenots.
2. Leaders.
   1. Catholics.
      1. Catharine de Medici.
      2. The Guises.
   2. Protestants.
      1. Henry Bourbon of Navarre.
      2. Prince Conde.
      3. Admiral Coligny.

*?. At one time they were about this size, but now only as large as W. Va. i. e. Holland and Belgium taken together.

OUTLINES OF GENERAL HISTORY   59

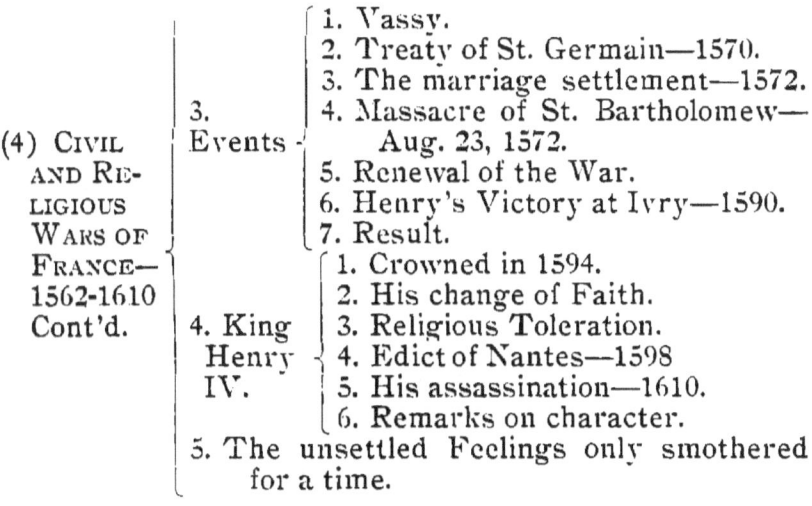

Chapter XVI.—England Under the Tudors. (1509-1603.)

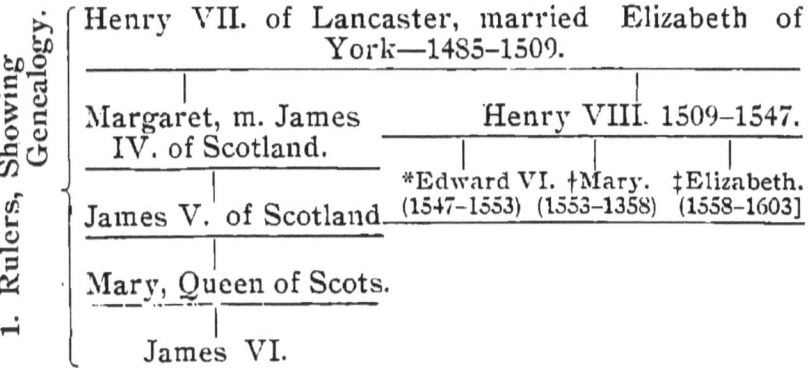

*Son of Jane Seymour.   †Daughter of Catharine, married Philip of Spain.
‡Daughter of Anne Boleyn.

2. Henry VIII.
- 1. His aid sought by Charles V. and Francis—1558-1603.
- 2. Battle of Flodden Field (Spurs.)
- 3. Revolt against Rome.
  - 1. Six articles of Faith.
  - 2. Change in Creed.
  - 3. Benevolences.
  - 4. "Morton's Fork."
- 4. Lollards.
- 5. Leaders.
  - 1. Colet.
  - 2. Erasmus.
  - 3. More.
- 6. His Wives.
  - 1. Catharine of Aragon.
  - 2. Anne Boleyn.
  - 3. Jane Seymour.
  - 4. Anne of Cleves.
  - 5. Catharine Howard.
  - 6. Catharine Parr.

3. Events of Other Reigns.
- 1. Acts of Supremacy and Uniformity. [ans.
- 2. Persecution of Puritans and Presbyteri-
- 3. Mary, Queen of Scots.
- 4. English lose Calais in reign of Mary.
- 5. The Invincible Armada defeated in the reign of Elizabeth, 1588.
- 6. Maritime and Colonial Enterprises.
- 7. Elizabeth's Favorites.
- 8. The Augustan Age of Literature.

4. The Beheadings of
- 1. Cranmer.
- 2. Cromwell.
- 3. More.
- 4. Wolsey.
- 5. Fisher.
- 6. Mary, Queen of Scots.
- 7. Earl of Leicester.
- 8. Earl of Essex.
- 9. Lady Jane Grey.
- 10. And others.

5. England's Position in the World.

Chapter XVII.—The Thirty Years War.
1618-1648

1. Causes.
   1. Troubles in Bohemia.
   2. Growing hatred between Protestants and Catholics.
   3. A dislike for the Emperor.
   4. Destruction of Churches, etc.

2. Leaders.
   1. Catholics.
      1. Ferdinand, Emperor.
      2. Wallenstein.
      3. Tilly.
      4. Peppenheim.
   2. Protestants
      1. Frederick, the Palatinate.
      2. Gustavus Adolphus, (King of Sweden.)
      3. Bernard of Weimar, (Swede.)
      4. Conde and Turenne, (French.)

3. Periods of the War.
   1. Bohemian Period—1618-23.
   2. Danish Period—1625-29—Peace of Lubeck.
   3. Swedish Period—1630—35.
   4. French Period—1635-48.

4. Important Battles.
   1. Madgeburg.
   2. Leipsic—1631.
   3. Lutzen—1632.
   4. Rocroi.
   5. Frieburg.
   6. Nordlingen—1634.
   7. Lens.

5. Treaty of Westphalia—1648.

6. Results.
   1. Amnesty to Political Offenders.
   2. Catholics and Protestants no longer have Ecclesiastical rights over each other.
   3. Each Prince sovereign in his own province.
   4. Switzerland and the Dutch Republic recognized as Independent.
   5. Sweden gets territory on the Baltic.
   6. France gets Alsace.
   7. Brandenburg's territory increased.

Chapter XVIII.—The Monarchy in France. (1610-1715.)

The Monarchy in France—1610-1715
- 1. Age of Richilieu—1622-42.
  - 1. Louis XIII, King—1610-43.
  - 2. Rochelle.
  - 3. Nobles humbled.
  - 4. Part of France in 30 yrs. War
  - 5. Object of Richilieu.
  - 6. Result.
- 2. Age of Louis XIV—1643-1715.
  - 1. Peace of Pyrennes—1659.
  - 2. His Ministers.
    - 1. Mazarin—1643-61.
    - 2. Colbert.
    - 3. Louvois.
    - 4. Luxembourg.
  - 3. His Wars.
    - 1. With Flanders—1667-68. Treaty of Aix-la Chapelle.
    - 2. With Holland—1672-79.
      - 1. Triple Alliance.
      - 2. Treaty Nimeguen
    - 3*. Of the Palatinate—1688-97.
      - 1. Holy Alliance.
      - 2. Peace Ryswick.
    - 4†. Spanish Succession—1701-14.
      - 1. Treaty of Utrecht.
      - 2. Radstadt.
  - 4. Generals.
    - 1. French.
      - 1. Turenne.
      - 2. Conde.
      - 3. Luxembourg.
      - 4. Vauban.
    - 2. Dutch and English.
      - 1. William of Orange.
      - 2. Marlborough.
      - 3. Eugene.

*Called in this country, "King William's War."
†Our "Queen Anne's War."

2. Age of Louis XIV— 1643-1715.— Cont'd.

5. Battles
1. Fleurus.
2. Steinkirk.
3. Neerwinden.
4. Blenheim.
5. Ramillies.
6. Oudenarde.
7. Malplaquet.
} English Victories.

6. His misfortunes and Death—Sept. 1, 1715.

3. The Augustan age of Literature in France.

4. The Court at Versailles.

Chapter XIX.—England under the Stuarts. (1603-1714.)

1. Table of Rulers showing Genealogy. (see p. 59.)

James VI of Scotland becomes James I. of England, (1603–1625.)

Charles I. (m Henrietta Maria. of France) (1625–1649.)   Elizabeth (m. Frederick of Palatine.)

Charles II. (1660–1685.)   James II. (1685–1689.)   Sophia, (m. Elector of Hanover.)

Mary m. William (of Orange) III (1689–1694.)   Anne (1702–1715.) (1689–1702.)   George I.

2. Reign of James I.
1. The Gunpowder Plot—1605.
2. Rise of Parliament—1610-40.
3. His Foreign Policy.
4. His Character.

3. Reign of Charles I
  1. The Long Parliament—1640-53.
  2. The Short Parliament.
  3. Civil War—1642-48.
     1. Causes
        1. "Divine Right" of Kings.
        2. Trouble with Parliament.
     2. Leaders
        1. King.
           1. He and his son.
           2. Prince Rupert.
        2. Parliament.
           1. John Hampden.
           2. Oliver Cromwell.
           3. Ireton.
        3. Battles.
           1. Edgehill—1643.
           2. Marston Moor—1644.
           3. Naseby—1645.
        4. Result.
  4. His Fate and Character.

4. The Commonwealth —1649-60
  1. Oliver Cromwell, Protector—1649-60.
  2. War in Ireland and Scotland.
  3. Dunbar and Worcester.
  4. War with Holland.
  5. Presbyterians and Quakers.
  6. Oliver's Death and Character.
  7. His Successor.
  8. The *Restoration*—1660.

5. Charles II's Reign
  1. The Reaction.
  2. Plague in London—1665.
  3. Great Fire—1666—(200,000 people destitute of homes.)
  4. War with Holland.
  5. Treaty of Dover in France—1670.
  6. Rye House and other Plots.
  7. The Test Act.
  8. Whigs and Tories.

6. James II's Reign and the Revolution.

7. William and Mary's Reign.
- 1. The Bill of Rights—1689.
- 2. Battle of Boyne in England.
- 3. Jacobite Plots.
- 4. House of Commons Supreme.
- 5. England aids the Palatinate in the War of Louis XIV against him. (see p. 62.)
- 6. His Death and Character—1702.

8. Queen Anne's Reign.
- 1. War of the Spanish Succession—1701-14.
- 2. Union of England and Scotland—1707.
- 3. Marlborough's (John Churchill) Victories.
- 4. The Last of the Stuarts.
- 5. Her Character.

Chapter XX.—Peter the Great and Charles XII. (1689-1725)

1. Rise of Russia
- 1. Sketch of Early History.
- 2. Past Rulers.
  - 1. Ivan the Terrible—1533-84.
  - 2. Feodor—1584-1598.
  - 3. Michael Romanoff—1613-89.
  - 4*. Peter the Great—1689-1725.
- 3. Its location.
  - 1. In Western Asia and Eastern Europe
  - 2. Occupies ½ of Europe and ⅓ of Asia

2. Peter the Great.
- 1. As a boy.
- 2. In Western Europe
- 3. His Reforms.
- 4. His Character.

3. Charles XII of Sweden.
- 1. As a boy.
- 2. His Enemies.
  - 1. Denmark.
  - 2. Poland.
  - 3. Russia.
  - 4. Prussia.
  - 5. Turks.
- 3. His Death—1718.
- 4. His Character.

4. Russia's War with Sweden.
- 1. Cause—Russia's Greed for Territory.
- 2. Some Battles.
  - 1. Narva—1706.
  - 2. Pultowa—1709.
  - 3. Frederickshall—1718.
- 3. Result.

*Notice that William III. came to the throne in England at this time, that Louis XIV began his War of the Palatinate, and we had our King William's War.

5. Further additions of Territory.
6. Founding of Petersburg.

Chapter XXI.—Rise of Prussia.—1640-1786.

1. Brandenburg and Frederick William—1640-1749.
2. How the Elector procured the title of King.
3. Reign of Frederick William I.—1713-40.
4. Reign of Frederick the Great. (1740-86.)
   1. Sketch of his Life.
   2. His Wars
      1. *Austrian Succession—1740-48.
         1. Dettingen.
         2. Fontenoy.
         3. Result.
      2. †The Seven Years War—1756-63.
         1. Cause.
         2. Allies against him.
            1. Austria.
            2. Russia.
            3. France.
            4. Poland.
            2. Saxony.
            6. Sweden.
         3. Important Battles.
            1. Rossback.
            2. Leuthen.
            3. Zorndorf.
            4. Kolin. (d)
            5. Kurnersdorf. (d)
            6. Leignitz.
            7. Torgau.
         4. Peace of Paris.
         5. Result.
   2. His W'rks
   3. His Government.
   4. Anecdotes and Character.

*King George's War in U. S.   †French and Indian War in U. S.

Chapter XXII.—England Under House of Hanover, 1714-1820.

1. Table of Rulers—(See p. 63.) George I. (1714-27.)

2. Reign of the Three Georges.
   George II. (1727-60.)
   *George III. (1760-20.)
   1. King's Loss of Influence.
   2. Continental Affairs.
   3. Wars of the Pretenders
      1. Old Pretender.
      2. Young Pretender.
      3. Culloden.
   4. The French and Indian War—1755-63.
      1. Braddock.
      2. Wolfe.
      3. Treaty of 1763.

3. Their Character.
   5. American Revolution—1775-83.
      1. Burgoyne.
      2. Cornwallis.
      3. Paris, 1783.
      4. Result.
   6. Independence of Ireland.

4. England Humbled.
   7. French Revolution.

Chapter XXIII.—French Revolution and France.

1. Previous History of France since 1715.
   1. Louis XVI.
   2. His Troubles.

2. Causes of the Revolution.
   1. Excessive Extravagance.
   2. Excessive Taxes on the Peasants.
   3. Burdensome Privileges of the Nobility.
   4. Growing Feeling of the People.
   5. The Influence of the American Revolution.
   6. The Writings of
      1. Voltaire.
      2. Rousseau.
      3. Corneille.
      4. Raynal.
      5. Heloctius.

*Grandson of George II.

OUTLINES OF GENERAL HISTORY

3. Periods of the Revolution.
- 1. States General to 1789.
  - 1. Paris mob.
  - 2. The Bastile.
- 2. Th Legislative Assembly—1791-92.
  - 1. Attack on Tuilleries.
  - 2. Battle of Valmy—1792.
- 4. The National Convention—1792-95.
  - 1. Louis XVI beheaded—1793
  - 2. *"Reign of Terror"*—June 2, 1793–July 27, 1794.
  - 3. Reactionary Period.
  - 5. French Successes.
- 5. The Directory—1795-1799.
  - 1. Napoleon Bonaparte at the Helm.
    - 1. Battles
      - 1. Lodi.
      - 2. Arcole.
      - 3. Mantua.
    - 2. Italian Campaign—1795-7.
      - 2. Opposing Generals.
        - 1. Bealieu.
        - 2. Wurmser.
        - 3. Alvincy.
      - 3. The Result.
      - 4. His marriage.
    - 3. Egyptian Campaign—1798-9.
      - 1. Battles.
        - 1. Pyramids.
        - 2. Aboukir bay.
        - 3. Aboukir (on land)
      - 2. His Return.
      - 3. Overthrows Directory.
      - 4. Treaty of Campo-Formio—1799.

3. Periods of the Revolution.
- 6. The Consulate—1799-1804.
  - 1. Second Italian campaign—1799-01.
    - 1. Marengo. [ville.
    - 2. Treaty of Lune-
    - 3. Result.
  - 2. German Campaign—1800-1802.
    - 1. Hohenlinden.
    - 2. Treaty of Amiens.
- 7. The Empire—1804-15.
  - 1. Austrian Campaign—1804-06.
    - 1. Ulm.
    - 2. Austerlitz.
  - 2. Prussian Campaign—1806.
    - 1. Jena.
    - 2. Auerstadt.

3. Periods of the Revolution—Cont'd.
- 7. The Empire—1804-15.—Cont'd.
  - 3. Russian Campaign—1807.
    1. Eylau.
    2. Friedland.
    3. Result.
    4. Tilsis Treaty.
  - 4. The Spanish Campaign—1808
    1. Continental System.
    2. Berlin Decree.
    3. Milan Decree.
  - 5. The 2d Austrian Campaign—1809.
    1. Aspern.
    2. Wagram.
    3. His 2d marriage.
  - 6. Second Spanish Campaign—1809-12
  - 7. Second Russian Campaign—1812.
    1. Borodino.
    2. Moscow.
    3. Results.
  - 8. All Europe in Arms—1812-14.
    1. Lutzen.
    2. Bautzen.
    3. Dresden.
    4. Leipsic.
  - 9. Abdication of Napoleon to Elba.
  - 10. Louis XVIII. placed on the Throne
- 8. The 100 Days in France
- 9. Napoleon's Return—1815
  1. Escape of Louis XVIII.
  2. To Arms again.
  3. Congress of Vienna.
  4. Waterloo, (June 18, 1815.)
  5. His Abdication to St. Helena.
  6. His Death and Character.

4. The Second Restoration—1815-48
- 1. Kings
  1. Louis XVIII.—1815-24.
  2. Charles X—1824-30.
  3. Louis Philippe—1830-48.
- 2. Events
  1. Revolution of the 3 days of July—1830.
  2. Dissensions and Party Strife.
  3. Revolution of 1848.

5. Second Republic—1848-52.
  1. The mobs of Paris—Louis leaves.
  2. Louis Napoleon becomes President
  2. Chamber of Deputies dissolved.

70　　　　　　OUTLINES OF GENERAL HISTORY

6. The Second Empire—1852-70.
- 2. His Wars.
  - 1. Louis Napoleon becomes Napoleon III.
  - 1. Crimean War—1853-56.
    - 1. England and France aid Turkey against Russia.
    - 2. Battles.
      - 1. Alma.
      - 2. Balaklava.
      - 3. Inkerman.
      - 4. Sabastopol.
    - 3. Treaty of Paris.
    - 4. Result.
  - 2. Austro-Sardinian War—1859-60.
    - 1. France helps Italy against Austria.
    - 2. Battles.
      - 1. Magenta.
      - 2. Solferino.
    - 3. Peace, Villa Franca.
    - 4. Result.
      - 1. Sardinia gets Lombardy and Modena.
      - 2. France gets Nice and Savoy.
      - 3. 9,000,000 free from Austria.
  - 3. Mexican War—1859.
  - 4. The Franco-Prussian War—1870-71.
    - 1. Causes
      - 1. Alsace-Lorraine.
      - 2. Spanish Crown.
    - 2. Leaders.
      - 1. Napoleon. } French.
      - 2. Bazaine. }
      - 3. Bismarck. } German.
      - 4. Von Moltke. }
    - 3. Battles.
      - 1. Weissenburg.
      - 2. Worth.
      - 3. Courcelles.
      - 4. Thionville.
      - 5. Gravelotte.
      - 6. Sedan.
      - 7. Metz.
    - 4. Peace.
    - 5. Result.
- 3. His Imprisonment
- 4. His Character.

OUTLINES OF GENERAL HISTORY 71

7. The Third Republic— 1871-1897.
- 1. The Presidents.
  1. M. Thiers—1871-73.
  2. Marshal McMahon—1873-79.
  3. M. Grevy—1879-87.
  4. M. Carnot—1887-94.
  5. M. Casimir-Perier—1894-95.
  6. M. Felix Faure—1895——.
- 2. Events.
  1. The Communists—1871.
  2. Growth of Education.
  3. The War Debt of 5,000,000,000 francs, promptly paid to Germany.
  4. The Finances.
  5. Assassination of Pres. Carnot—1894.
  6. Resignation Pres. Casimir-Perier—1895.
  7. National Growth since 1871.

8. *Leaders and Generals of this Period.* (see "p.")

Chapter XXIV—England Under House of Hanover 1820-1897.

1. Genealogy of the Rulers.

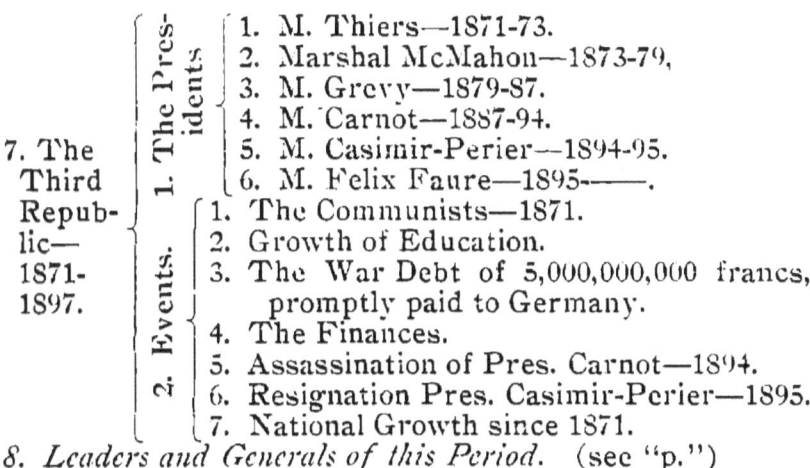

George III. (see p. 63.)
George IV. William IV. Edward of Kent
(1820-30.) (1830-37.)
                          Victoria.
                          (1837——.)

2. Events of Geo. IV's Reign.
  1. Corn Laws.
  2. Repeal of Test Act—1828.
  3. Fires and Famines.

3. Reign of William IV
  1. 1st Locomotive, Liverpool to Manchester 1830
  2. First Reform Bill, 1832.
  3. Emancipation Bill, 1833.
  4. The Chartists and Revolution of 1848.

"p"
1. Marat.   5. Necker.   9. Massena.   13. Napoleon I.   17. Carnot.
2. Mirabeau.   6. Barras.   10. Kleber.   14. Napoleon III 18. Faure.
3. Danton.   7. Kellerman. 11. Augereau.   15. Bazaine.
4. Robespierre 8. Jourdan.   12. Ney.   16. Thiers.

4. Victoria's Reign.
{
1. Anti-Corn Law League—1839.
2. Cobden Free Trade Club.
3. Cheap Postage—1840—Roland Hill.
4. First World's Fair at London—1851.
5. Crimean War (see France p. 70.)
6. Indian Munity—1857.
7. Cotton Famine—1860-65.
8. Reform Bill of 1867.
9. Compulsory School System—1870.
10. Irish Land Titles Arranged—1870-71.
11. Religious Tests abolished in the Universities—1871
12. Voting by Ballot introduced—1872.
13. The Queen becomes Empress of India—1876.
14. England checks Russia's greed for Constantinople —1878.
15. Mahdi's Rebellion in Egypt—1885.
16. Stanley in search of Dr. Livingston in Africa—1888.
17. Free Education in Scotland—1889.
18. Kindergarten and Manual Training School introduced.
19. The Retirement of Gladstone—1896.
20. The Venezuelan affair—1896.

Chapter XXV—Other Modern Nations.

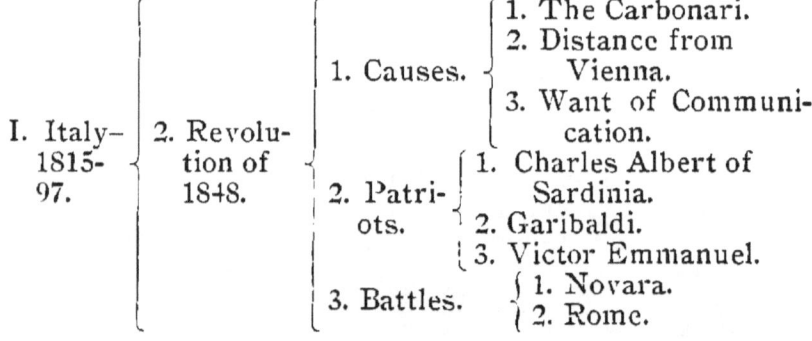

I. Italy
1815-97
- 3. Assists England and France in the Crimean War.
- 4. Revolution of 1858-9 (see France p. 70.)
- 5. Dawn of Freedom.
- 6. Victor Emmanuel II becomes King—1861-78.
  - 1. Italy helps Prussia in 1866.
  - 2. Gains Venice and Verona.
  - 3. Gets Rome in 1870, and it is the Capital.
- 7. King Humbert I. 1878.
  - 1. States of the Church added.
  - 2. The Pope now a Spiritual Power.
  - 3. Troubles in Abyssinia.
  - 4. Her Growth.

II. Germany—1806-97
- 1. Holy Roman Empire ends 1806.
- 2. A Confederation of 39 States with Austria at its head—1815.
- 3. Prussia recovers the territory wrested from her by Napoleon.
- 4. The Holy Alliance { 1. Russia. 2. Austria. 3. Prussia. } 1815.
- 5. The Zollverein—1828.
- 6. Revolution of 1848.
  - 1. Demand for Unity.
  - 2. Berlin.
  - 3. Patriots
    - 1. Frederick Wm. IV.
    - 2. Bismarck.
    - 3. Kossuth.
  - 4. Opposing Leaders.
    - 1. Ferdinand of Austria.
    - 2. Metternich.
    - 3. Francis Joseph.
    - 4. "The Hangman."
  - 5. Result.
- 7. War with Denmark—1864.
  - 1. Prussia helps Austria.
  - 2. They take Schleswig-Holstein.

II. Germany.—
1806-97

    8. Seven weeks War—1866.
- 1. Prussia against Austria.
- 2. Battle of Sadowa.
- 3. Peace of Prague.
- 4. Result (Austria defeated.)

    9. The North German Confederation.

    10. Emperors
- 1. William I—1871-88.
- 2. Frederick—1888.
- 3. William II—1888—.

    11. Ministers.
- 1. Caprivi.
- 2. Bismarck.

    12. Austria Grants Reforms.

    13. Francis Joseph becomes King of Hungary —1867.

III. Russia—
1801-97

1. Rulers since Peter the Great
- 1. Catherine—1725-62.
- 2. Catherine II—1762-96.

2. Events under Alexander I— 1801-25.
- 1. The Holy Alliance of { Russia, Prussia and Austria.
- 2. Trouble with the Liberals.
- 3. Conspiracies.

3. Reign of Nicholas I—1825-55
- 1. A Terrible Autocrat.
- 2. Aids Greece against Turkey in 1828.
- 3. Revolution in Poland—1830.
- 4. Added to Russia - 1832.
- 5. Assists Austria to crush Hungary in 1848.
- 6. The Crimean War, (see France)

4. Reign of Alexander II—1855—81.
- 1. Popular Reforms.
- 2. Emancipation of Slaves—1858-63.
- 3. Rebellion in Poland—1863.
- 4. *War with Turkey—1877-78.
- 5. Treaty of Berlin and Results.
- 6. Siberian Exiles—1879-80.
- 7. Assassination of the Czar—March 13, 1881.

*Turkey loses Roumania, Servia, Montenegro and protection of Bulgaria in this war.

III. Russia—
1801-97
Cont'd.
- 5. Alexander III—1881-85
  1. Censorship of the Press.
  2. His assassination—1895.
  3. Character.
- 6. Nicholas II—1895.
  1. Better man than his Predecessor.
  2. Condition of the People.

IV. Less Important Countries.
- I. The Netherlands.
  1. Throw off the French Yoke—1812
  2. Belgium and Holland united—1815
  3. *Belgians Rebel in 1830.
  4. Leopold made King of Belgium and William IV, King of Holland.
  5. Present Queen of Holland—Wilhelmina.
- II. Turkey.
  1. Its Former Greatness.
  2. Decline since the Battle of Lepanto 1571.
  3. See Russia for events of 1821-56-78.
  4. Armenian massacres—1895-96.
- III. Greece.
  1. Revolts against Turkey—1821.
  2. Marco Bozzaris, the patriot.
  3. Allies of Greece.
  4. Battle of Navarino—1827.
  5. Georgias I. of Denmark elected King.
  6. War with Turkey over Candia—1897.
- IV. Japan.
  1. Glimpses of Early History
     1. Rule of the Jemmu—660 B. C.
     2. Buddhism—600 B. C.
     3. The Shogun—1192.
  2. Treaty with U. S.—1854.
  3. Revolution of 1868.
  4. Restoration of the Mikado.
  5. Conquered by the Portugese who were expelled in the 16th Century—*Influence*.
  6. The Senate—1875.
  7. Other assemblies—1879.
  8. A Constitutional Monarchy.
  9. Educational Progress.
  10. War with China—1894-95.
  11. The Result.

*Notice that numerous Revolutions occurred in 1820-1830-1848.

IV. Less Important Countries. Cont'd. — V. Spain.
1. Revolution of 1820.
2. The Spanish obtain a written Constitution.
3. Loses Territory in Italy—1848-59.
4. Loses South American countries and Mexico—1819-30.
5. Rebellion of Cuba and Phillipine Islands —1896-98.

Chapter XXVI.—Great Men of Centuries.

No.	Century.	Names.	Chief Work or Masterpieces.	Character or Profession.	Language or Nationality.
1	16th	Francis Bacon	"Novum Organum"	Author and Scientist	English.
2		Copernicus	Rotation of the earth	Philosopher	Italian.
3		Galileo	"System of the World"	Philosopher	Greek.
4		Thomas More	"Utopia"	Author	English.
5		Hugo Grotius	International Law	Lawyer and Author	Latin.
6		Michael Angelo (Buonarroti)	Work on St. Peter's Church	Sculptor and Painter	Italian.
7		Raphael	Decorates the Vatican	Painter	Italian.
8		Titian	"The Assumption"	Painter	Italian.
9		Albert Durer	Inventor of Etching and Wood Engraving	Engraver and Sculptor	German.
10		Edmund Spencer	"Faerie Queene"	Poet	English.
11		Wm Shakespeare	"Hamlet" and 36 Dramas	Poet	English.
12		Philip Sidney	"Arcadia"	Poet and Author	English.
13		Sir Walter Raleigh	"History of the World"	Author and Courtier	English.
14		Cervantes	"Don Quixote"	Author	Spanish.
15		Rabelais	"Life of Pantagruel"	Priest and Author	French.
16		Montaigne	"Essays"	Author	French.
17		Aristo	"Orlando-Furioso"	Poet	German.
18		Tasso	"Jerusalem Delivered"	Poet	Italian.
19		Tyco Brahe	Discoveries in Science	Astronomer	Danish.
20		Holbein	"Dance of Death"	Painter	German.
21	17th	Hobbes	"Leviathan"	Historian and Philosopher	English.

No.	Century	Names.	Chief Work or Masterpieces.	Character or Profession.	Language or Nationality.
22	17th	Isaac Newton	"Principia"..	Scientist and Mathematician	English.
23		Liebnitz.........	Philosophy.	Scientist...	German.
24		Rubens	"Descent of the Cross."............	Painter	Dutch.
25		Vandyck..	Court Painter for Charles I	Painter....	Dutch. ....
26		Poussin......	"The Last Supper"	Painter	French
27		B. E. Murillo	"The marriage of St. Catharine".....	Painter	Spanish.
28		Ben Johnson..	"Every Man in His Humor"...............	Author.........	English.
29		Kepler........	Laws of Motion......	Philosopher	German.
30		William Harvey.........	Discovers the Circulation of the Blood	Physician...	English.
31		Descartes....	Philosophical W'ks	Author.........	French.
32		*Duke of Marlborough (John Churchill...	"Hero of Blenhem."	General......	English
33		Corneille	"Cid."...................	Poet	French.
34		John Milton..	"Paradise Lost."...	Epic Poet...	English.
35		Jeremy Taylor....	"Holy Living and Dying."............	Author	English.
36		La Fontaine...	"Fables".	Author.........	French.
37		Moeire.	Wrote Comedies......	Dramatist...	French.
38		Bousset	Wrote Sermons........	Orator and Preacher.	French.
39		John Bunyan..	"Pilgrim's Progress."	Preacher and Author	English.
40		John Dryden.	"Religio Laici."...	Poet, etc...	English.
41		Racine, }	"Telemaque.".....	Author.........	French,
42		Fenelon. }			
43	18th	Benjamin Franklin...	Invents Lightning Rod. Introduces Newspapers.........	Philosopher Printer, Statesman	American.
44		Linnæus......	Botany.............	Author.........	Swedish.
45		D'Alembert...	"Memoir of the Integral Calculus."	Scientist...	French.

*Many important General's names are omitted in this table because they are more properly treated in the outlines of the different wars.

No.	Century	Names.	Chief Work or Masterpieces.	Character or Profession.	Language or Nationality.
46	18th	John Hunter	Works on Anatomy.	Scientist	Scotch.
47		Kant	Metaphysics	Philosopher	German.
48		Galvani	Invents Electric Battery	Inventor and Scientist	Italian.
49		Sir Wm. Herschel	Discovers the Planet, *Uranus*	Astronomer	English.
50		Adam Smith	"Wealth of Nations."	Author and Scientist	Scotch.
51		Lavoisier	Chemistry	Chemist	French.
52		J. Bentham	"Utilitarianism."	Philosopher	English.
53		La Place	"Mecanique Celestia."	Philosopher and Astronomer	French.
54		Jonathan Swift	"Gulliver's Travels."	Author	English.
55		Joseph Addison	"The Spectator."	Editor and Author	English.
56		Alexander Pope	"Essay on Man."	Poet	English.
57		Montesquieu	"L'Esprit des Lois." (The Spirit of Laws.)	Author and Thinker	French.
58		Voltaire	"Henriade"—"Charles XII."	Author and Free-thinker	French.
59		Buffon	"Histoire Naturelle."	Author and Scientist	French.
60		Fielding	"Tom Jones."	Author	English.
61		Sam Johnson	"Rasselas"—"Dictionary".	Author	English.
62		David Hume	"History of England".	Historian	English.
63		Rousseau	"Emile".	Author and Educator	Swiss.
64		Oliver Goldsmith	"Vicar of Wakefield"	Author	English.
65		G. E. Lessing	"Laocoon".	Author	German.
66		Edmund Burke	"Essay on Sublime and Beautiful".	Orator and Rhetorician	English.

No.	Century	Names	Chief Work or Masterpieces.	Character or Profession.	Language or Nationality.
67	15th	Edward Gibbon	"Rise and Decline of the Roman Empire"	Historian	English.
68		Robert Burns	"Cotter's Saturday Night".	Poet	Scotch.
69		J. C. F. Schiller	"William Tell".	Poet	German.
70		Joshua Reynolds	Pres. Royal Academy	Artist and Painter	English.
71		Geo. F. Handel	"The Messiah"	Musical Composer	German.
72		Joseph Haydn	"The Creation"	Musician and Orator	Italian.
73		Benjamin West	Painter at Royal Academy.	Painter	American.
74		Johann Mozart	"Don Giovanni"	Musician	German.
75		Antonio Canova	"Venus and Adonis".	Sculptor	Italian.
76		James Brindley	Invents Canals	Inventor	English.
77		James Hargraves	Spinning Jenny and Card Machine.	Inventor	English.
78		Josiah Wedgwood	Invents Queensware	Inventor	English.
79		Richard Arkwright	Cotton manufacture.	Inventor	English.
80		James Watt	Steam Engine	Inventor	English.
81		*Robert Fulton	Steamboat	Inventor	American.
82		Joseph Jacquard	Looms to Weave Figures	Inventor	French.
83		George Washington	Frees his Country	General	American.
84	19th	Nicolo Paganini	Celebrated Violinist	Musician	Italian.
85		Alex. M. Humbolt	"Kosmos"	Scientist and Author	German.
86		†Georges Cuvier	Natural History	Scientist	Swiss.

*James Rumsey, of W. Va., is also said to be the inventor of the Steamboat.
†He had an emminent brother scientist, Frederick.

No.	Century	Names.	Chief Work or Masterpieces.	Character or Profession.	Language or Nationality.
87	19th	Sir Humphrey Davey	Invents Safety Matches for lamps	Inventor	English.
88		Francois D. Arago	Discovers Diameters of the Planets—Polariscope	Astronomer and Artist.	French.
89		Sir Wm. Hamilton	Metaphysical Writer	Author and Philosopher	English.
90		Michael Faraday	Physics and Philosophy	Author and Scientist	English.
91		Auguste Comte	Philosophical Works	Author	French.
92		Baron Liebig	Physiology	Author and Doctor	German.
93		U. J. J. Leverrier	Discovers the planet Neptune	Astronomer	French.
94		John Tyndall	"Water, Electricity and Light."	Philosopher	English.
95		L. J. R. Agassiz	Natural History	Scientist	Swiss.
96		Jno. W. Goethe	"Faust."	Poet	German.
97		J. P. Richter	Anatomy	Author and Scientist.	German.
98		William Wordsworth	"The Excursion."	Poet	English.
99		Walter Scott	"Ivanhoe"—"Marmion."	Novelist and Poet	English.
100		Thomas Campbell	"Gertrude of Wyoming."	Poet	English.
101		Lord Byron	"Child Harold's Pilgrimage."	Poet	English.
102		S. T. Coleridge	Essays, Poems, etc.	Poet and Author	English.
103		Beranger	Satires upon the Gout	Poet	French.
104		F. P. G. Guizot	"History of Civilization."	Author	French.
105		Thos. Carlyle	"French Revolution."	Author	English.
106		W. H. Prescott	"Conquest of Mexico."	Historian	American.

No.	Century.	Names.	Chief Work or Masterpieces.	Character or Profession.	Language or Nationality.
107	19th	Washington Irving	"Life of Washington."	Historian	American.
108		M. Thiers	Pres. of France	Statesman and Historian.	French.
109		T. B. McCaulay	"History of England."	Author	English.
110		George Bancroft	"History of the U. S."	Historian	American.
111		Victor Hugo	"Les Miserables."	Novelist	French.
112		R. W. Emerson	"Essays."	Author	American.
113		Nathaniel Hawthorne	"Scarlet Letter."	Novelist	American.
114		Alfred Tennyson	"Idylls of the King."	Poet	English.
115		W. M. Thackeray	"Vanity Fair"	Novelist	English.
116		Chas. Dickens	"Nicholas Nickleby."	Novelist	English.
117		J. Fenimore Cooper	"Leather Stocking Tales."	Novelist	American.
118		Albert Thorwaldsen	"Christ and the Twelve Apostles."	Sculptor	Danish.
119		Ludwig Beethoven	"Mount of Olives."	Musical Composer.	German.
120		Jos. Turner	Landscape Painter.	Artist	English.
121		Horace Vernet	"The Bombardment of Madrid."	Painter	French.
122		G. Rosini	"William Tell."	Musical Composer.	Italian.
123		G. Meyerbeer.			
124			Astonished people by his talent when only six y'rs old.	Musician	German.
125		Jacob Mendelssohn	"Oratorios."	Musician	German.
126		Gustave Dore.	Illustrations for Don Quixote	Artist	French.
		Sir Isaac Brunel	Engineer, Thames Tunnel.	Inventor	English.

No.	Century.	Names.	Chief Work or Masterpieces.	Character or Profession.	Language or Nationality.
127	19th	Geo. Stephenson	The Locomotive	Inventor	English.
128		L. J. M. Daguerre	How to fix Images	Inventor and Artist.	French.
129		S. F. B. Morse	Electric Telegraph.	Inventor.	American.
130		Thos. A. Edison	Phonograph	Inventor	American.
131		A. Graham Bell	Telephone.	Inventor	American.
132		*Eli Whitney.	Cotton Gin	Inventor	American.
133		A. Lincoln	President during Civil War in U. S.	Statesman	American.
134		James G. Blaine	Sec. of State under Pres. Harrison	Orator	American.
135		Elias Howe	Sewing Machine.	Inventor	American.
136		Edward Jenner	Discovers and introduces Vaccination.	Physician	English.
137		Edwin Forrest	Patriarch of his Country	Actor and Tragedian.	American.
138		Charles Goodyear	Invents Vulcanized India Rubber	Inventor	American.
139		Charles G. Brush	Invents the Arc Light Lamp	Inventor	American.
140		William E. Sawyer	Incandescent Carbon Lamp	Inventor	American.
141		John A. Roebling	Designed the East River Suspension Bridge	Architect	American.

*Lived in this Century, but his invention was in 1792.

Chapter XXVII.—Historical Pseudonyms and Sayings.

1. "The Snow King"—Gustavus Adolphus.
2. "The Winter King"—Palatine Frederick, son-in-law of James I.
3. "The Marathon of Switzerland"—Morgarten.
4. "The Sea Beggars"—The Dutch.
5. "The first man in Europe and the second in France"—Louis XIII.
6. "The Nephew of his Uncle"—Augustus.
7. "First Gentleman in Europe"—Geo. IV. of England.
8. "Little Man in Red Stockings"—Emperor Leopold of Germany.
9. "Last of the Tribunes"—Rienzi.
10. "Madman of the North"—Chas. XII. of Sweden.
11. "The Silent One"—William I. of Netherlands.
12. "The Lost Dauphin"—Louis XVII. who suffered in prison two years and died.
13. "First of the Stuarts"—James VI. of Scotland.
14. "The Conqueror of Crecy"—Edward III. of Scotland.
15. "The Merry Monarch"—Chas. II. of England.
16. "The Conqueror of Blenheim"—Marlborough.
17. "The Philosopher"—Marcus Aurelius Autonius.
18. "The Pretender"—James III., son of James II.
19. "The Young Pretender"—Charles III., son of Jas. II.
20. "Battle of the Nations"—Leipsic.
21. "Best of the Georges"—George IV. of England.
22. "King Hal"—Henry VIII. of England.
23. "Citizen King"—Louis Phillipe of France.
24. "The Great Prussian Drill Sergeant"—Carlyle says, Frederick William I.
25. "Conqueror of Agincourt"—Henry V. of England.
26. "Queen Bess"—Elizabeth of England.
27. "Iron Duke"—Count Von Moltke of Prussia.
28. "Greatest of the Plantagenets"—Richard I. of Eng.

29. "King of Bourges"—Charles VII. of France.
30. "Good Queen Anne"—Anne Stuart of England.
31. "The Virgin Queen"— } Elizabeth of England.
32. "The Napoleon of Peace"—
33. "King of the French"—Louis Phillipe of Orleans.
34. "Prisoner of Ham"—Napoleon III.
35. "Grand Monarch"—Louis XIV. of France.
36. "Eugenie"—Empress of Napoleon III.
37. "The Do Nothing Kings"—Merovingian *line of France.
38. "Corporal Violet"—Napoleon.
39. "Hero of Rocroi"—Conde of France.
40. "The Sailor King"—William IV. of England.
41. "Pride's Purge"—The soldiers under Col. Pride that shut Presbyterians out of Parliament.
42. "Hero of Marston Moor"—Oliver Cromwell.
43. "The Ironsides"—Cromwell's Troops.
44. "The Black Hole"—Calcutta Prison.
45. "The Black Prince"—Edward I. of England.
46. "Father Fritz"—Frederick I. of Prussia.
47. "The Sick Man"—Sultan of Turkey.
48. "The Horace of France"—Boileau.
49. "Upholsterer of Notre Dame"—Luxembourg.
50. "Hero of the Red Shirt"—Garibaldi of Italy,
51. "The Flower of Chivalrie"—E. Spenser says this of Sir Philip Sidney.
52. "The King Maker"—Earl of Warwick, England.
53. "I am the State"—Louis XIV.
54. "The Scourge of God"—Attila the Hun.
55. "Wisest Fool in Europe"—James I. of England, (Author, Sully of France.)
56. "Last of the Knights"—Maximilian of Germany.
57. "After Me the Deluge"—Louis XV.
58. "The Citizen King"—Louis Phillippe.
59. "The Little Corporal"—Napoleon.
60. "The Sword of Rome"—Marcellus.

*Line, here means family.

61. "Book of the Dead," } Phahtokeps Ritual for the
62. "Dispensary of the Soul" } Soul after Death.
63. "The Egyptian Alexander the Great"—Thotmes III.
64. "Daughter of Sidon and Mother of Carthage"—Tyre (a city.)
65. "School of Greece"—Athens.
66. "Eye of Greece"—Corinth.
67. "The Seven-hilled City"—Rome.
68. "Hundred Gate Thebes"—Thebes of Egypt.
69. "The Religious Conqueror"—Constantine.
70. "The False Smerdis"—Gomates of Persia.
71. "The Egyptian Iliad"—Epic of Pentaur.
72. "The Sacred Mount"—Mons Sacer in Rome.
73. "Eldest Daughter of the Empire"—Venice in Italy.
74. "The Lost Tribes"—Ten tribes of the Israelites.
75. "Pearl of the East"—Princess Roxana of Persia.
76. "The Third Founder of Rome"—Caius Marius.
77. "The Blind Bard"—Homer.
78. "The Lame old Schoolmaster"—Tyrtaeus.
79. "The Theban Eagle"—Pindar.
80. "The Attic Bee"—Sophocles.
81. "The Mantuan Bard"—Virgil.
82. "The Light of Mankind"—Christ.
83. "The Lesbian Nightingale"—Sappho.
84. "Father of History"—Herodotus.
85. "The Great Commoner"—William Pitt.
86. "Aaron the Just"—Haroun-al-Raschid.
87. "Grand old Man"—W. E. Gladstone.
88. "The Washington of S. A."—Gen. Simon Bolivar.
89. "The Religious Conqueror"—Tiglath Pileser I.
90. "Hero of the Arabian Nights"—Haroun-al-Raschid.
91. "Conqueror of Babylon"—Inscription on Tiglathinins' Ring.
92. "The Conqueror of Babylon"—Cyrus of Persia.
93. "The Honest King"—Victor Emmanuel II.
94. "Delenda est Carthago"—Cato the Censor—said it of Carthage.

95. "Master, remember the Athenians"—Darius had his servant repeat this to him.
96. "The Rich King"—Croesus.
97. "Et tu, Brute"—Cæsar to Brutus.
98. "Head of the Army" (in Eng.)—Napoleon's Last Words.
99. "My Work is Done"—Cromwell's Last Words.
100. "I am the Rear Guard of the Grand Army"—Marshal Ney of France.
101. "Ah! Carthage, I behold thy doom"—Hannibal.
102. "Defender of the Faith"—Henry VIII.
103. "Thank God, I have done my duty"—Lord Nelson's Last Words.
104. "The Three Days of July"—Revolution of 1830 in France.
105. "Not angles, but angels"—Gregory said it of the English slaves.
106. "The 10,000 Immortals"—Part of Xerxes' Guards.
107. "Laws Written in Blood"—Draco's Laws for Athens.
108. "Rape of the Sabines"—Capture of wives by the Romans.
109. "The First Triumvirate"—Cæsar, Pompey and Crassus.
110. "The Second Triumvirate"—Augustus, Anthony and Lepidus.
111. "To free men, threats, have no power"—Cicero of Rome.
112. "Veni, vidi, vici"—Cæsar.
113. "I will send one of my old boots to govern you"— Charles XII.
114. "You are a bad imitation of Ulysses"—Solon to Pisistratus.
115. "Thou hast saved Rome but lost thy son"—Coriolanus to his mother.
116. "Morton's Fork"—System of begging for the church.
117. "The Divine Right of Kings"—Claimed by the Stuarts of England, and Bourbons, of France.

118. "The Ayrshire Plowman"—Robert Burns.
119. "A Novel without a Hero"—Thackeray's Vanity Fair.
120. "George Eliot"—Mary Ann Evans.
121. "In 1806 the 120th of the Cæsars became only Francis II., of Austria"—Francis held the Title of Cæsar of the Western Roman Empire, but Napoleon blotted the Empire out.
122. "The Ladies' Peace"—Treaty between Francis I., of France and Chas. V., of Germany, concluded by the King's mother and Emperor's Aunt.
123. "Better a drowned land than a lost land"—The cry of the Dutch when Leyden was besieged by the Spanish in 1574. They loosened the dykes.
124. "I do not intend to blush like Sigismund"—Charles V. when urged to break his pledge of safe conduct promised Martin Luther.
125. "Some bids are too big for any cage"—Ney was to bring back Napoleon to Paris in an iron cage, but fell into his arms.
126. "Varus, give me back my Legions"—Augustus, after defeat of Romans, 9 A. D.
127. "'Tis a sharp medicine, but a cure for all ills"—Walter Raleigh, when he felt the edge of the Executor's axe.
128. "Had I but served my God with half the zeal I served my country, he would not have given me over in my gray hairs"—Thomas Wolsey, Henry VIII's. prime minister, after incurring the King's displeasure.
129. "The Five Good Emperors"—(1) Nerva, (3) Trajan, (3) Hadrian, (4) Antonius Pius, (5) Marcus A. Antonuis.
130. "If you could see the cabbage I have planted you would never ask me to remount the throne"—Diocletian writing to Maximian who desired they should again become Emperors.
131. "With such soldiers I could conquer the world"—Pyrrhus said this of the Romans, his enemies.

132. "The Elgin Marbles"—Mythical Sculptures sent from Athens to London by English.
133. "Temple of the Sphinx"—The human-headed Lion Rock 190 feet, near Ghizeh.
134. "The Four Great Schools of Philosophy."—1. Academic; 2. Peripatetic; 3. Epicurean; 4. Stoic.
135. "I pride myself that no Athenian has ever had occasion to mourn on my account"—Pericles.
136. "His wisdom surpassed that of all the children of the East and of Egypt."—Solomon, the last King of Judea.
137. "It is easier to turn the Sun from its course than Fabricus from the path of honor"—Pyrrhus, the Greek General.
138. "The Cincinnatus of the West"—Lord Byron's Title for Washington.
139. "Lion of the North"—Gustavus Adolphus.
140. "Would that the people of Rome had but one neck, so I could cut it off at a single blow"—Emperor Caligula.
141. "I knew these Swedes would beat us at first, but in the end they will teach us how to beat them"—Peter the Great after the battle of Narva.
142. The King that "ate grass like an ox"—Nebuchednezzar.
143. "Who kept the Bridge in the brave days of old"—Horatius of early Rome.
144. "Madman of the North"—Charles XII., of Sweden.
145. "The Last of the Greeks"—Philopoemon.

Chapter XXVIII.—Creasey's Decisive Battles.

No.	NAME OF BATTLE	PARTIES FIGHTING	No. TROOPS ENGAGED	GENERALS	DATE	RESULT
1	Marathon	Athenians	10,000	Miltiades	490 B. C.	Athenian Victory.
		Persians	100,000	Datis & Artaphernes		
2	Syracuse	Syracusans and allies		Gylippus, Demosthenes	413 B. C.	Athenians Defeated.
		Athenians		Nicias		
3	Arbela	Greeks	35,000	Alexander	331 B. C.	Persians Defeated.
		Persians	70,000	Darius		
4	Metaurus	Romans		Livius and Nero	207 B. C.	Roman Victory.
		Carthaginians		Hasdrubal		
5	Winfield-Lippe	Germanic Tribes	30,000 (?)	Arminius	9 A. D.	Romans Defeated.
			15,000	Varus		
6	Chalons	Romans and Visigoths		Theodoric and Aetius	451 A. D.	Huns Defeated.
		Huns		Attila		
7	Tours	Franks and Gauls		Charles Martel	732	Mohamedans Defeated. (375,000 killed.)
		Mohammedans		Abderrahan		
8	Hastings	Normans	60,000	William	1066	Normans Victorious.
		Saxons	40,000	Harold		
9	Orleans	French		Joan of Arc	1429	French Victory.
		English		Ghiddsdale		
10	Armada	English	17,000	Drake, Howard & Raleigh	1588	English Victory.
		Spanish	32,000	M. Sidonia		
11	Blenheim	English	56,000	Marlborough and Eugene	1704	English Victory.
		French and allies	60,000	Tallard and Marsine		
12	Pultowa	Russians	60,000	Peter the Great	1709	Russian Victory.
		Swedes	24,000	Charles XII.		
13	Saratoga	Americans	10,000	Gates and Arnold	1777	English Defeated.
		English	6,000	Burgoyne		
14	Valmy	French	60,000	Dumouriez and Kellerman	1792	French Victory.
		Prussians and allies	125,000	Duke of Brunswick		
15	Waterloo	English and allies	120,000	Duke of Wellington	1815	French Defeated.
		French	60,000	Napoleon Bonaparte		

Chapter XXIX.—Ancient History Recreations.

I. Questions on Egypt.

1. When and by whom was Egypt founded?
2. Describe the Hyksos and tell of their reign.
3. What Pharaohs built the pyramids? Who "refused to let the Israelites go?"
4. Name the rival cities and tell of their rise and decline.
5. To what different countries has Egypt been subjected?
6. What may be said briefly of Egyptian education and and religion?
7. For what are they noted?

II. Questions on China and India.

8. For what are these people noted?
9. State the chief characteristics of their education and religion.
10. Who was Confucius? Chewangte?
11. Name the earliest dates in each country of which there is a record.
12. How did they regard other nations?

III. Babylonia–Assyria.

13. What date marks the rise of Babylonia and Assyria?
14. Who was the first King of Assyria?
15. By whom was Babylon founded and when?
16. Give a brief description of Babylon, comparing its size with the present size of London.
17. Name three of Babylon's most noted rulers.
18. Name the rival cities.
19. Explain the Biblical quotation, "The hand writing on the wall."

IV. Phœnicia and Judea.

20. For what were the Phœnicians noted?
21. When does the history of this nation begin?
22. Name the rival cities.
23. Where is Carthage? By whom founded? When?
24. What is the earliest date in Hebrew History.

25. What was the "Exodus?" When did it occur?
26. Name the greatest rulers of Judea.
27. Give the account of the division of the monarchy.
28. In what condition are the Hebrews today?

V. Medo-Persia.

29. How did Media and Persia become one nation?
30. What Persian King had Daniel thrown into the "den of lions?"
31. Explain the saying, "As unchangeable as the laws of the Medes and Persians."
32. Describe the Persian court.
33. Name three of the greatest rulers.
34. Give dates of Persia's rise, zenith and decline.
35. What religions had their birth in Persia?

VI. Greece.

36. Who were the first inhabitants of Greece?
37. Recite the legend of the Trojan War.
38. What classes of people were there in Greece?
39. Name the three great law-givers of Greece.
40. Define the words tyrant and slave as formerly used.
41. What was ostracism?
42. When, where and by whom was the first decisive battle of the world fought, and what was the result?
43. Who pitted the largest army the world ever saw against Greeks? Where did he meet with unexpected opposition? Where finally defeated?
44. Who was Pericles?
45. What enabled Athens to withstand such a long siege in the Peloponnesian war?
46. What was "The retreat of Ten Thousand?"
47. Who organized the Macedonian phalanx? Give a sketch of his life.
48. What became of Alexander's Kingdom after his death?
49. When did Greece become a Roman province?
50. Note the contrasts in the education of the Spartans and Athenians.

51. Name four Greek historians.
52. Name four poets.
53. Name four of each of the leading orators, painters, sculptors and philosophers.
54. Name the four great schools of philosophy, giving authors and the dates of the founding of each.
55. For what *one* thing were the Grecians most renowned?
56. What cities were rivals?
57. Make a list of some of the greatest generals in chronological order.
58. What was the nature of their religion?
59. How did it in the modern era pass under control of Turkey, and how did it become free?
60. Who was Marco Bozzaris?
61. When and what was the result of the battle of Missolonghi?

VII. ROME.

62. When and by whom was Rome founded?
63. What two classes of people figured in Roman History?
64. Who was Cincinnatus? Horatio?
65. Give a short sketch of the early Brutus.
66. How many Kings had Rome in her early days?
67. Give their names.
68. What Carthaginian general invaded Rome? With what success did he meet?
69. Give a short sketch of each of the following men: Marius, Sulla and Cataline.
70. Who constituted the first triumvirate, and when was it formed?
71. State the results of the triumvirate, briefly.
72. Of whom was the second triumvirate composed, and when was it formed?
73. State the character of the men.
74. How was Anthony captured by his royal enemy?
75. What date marks the beginning of Imperial Rome?
76. Who is the central figure in all history, and who was emperor when he was born?

77. Who said, "I would that the Romans had but one neck so I might cut it off at a single blow?"
78. Who lighted his gardens with "human torches?"
79. Name the five "Good Emperors."
80. What and when was the age of the Thirty Tyrants?
81. How was Constantine converted to Christianity?
82. When was the empire divided?
83. Name the three great barbaric leaders who invaded Rome.
84. Who was the last Roman Monarch?
85. Name four of each of the leading poets, orators, historians and philosophers.
86. Describe a gladiatiorial combat.
87. Name the six successive world empires.
88. Of what did the Roman Education consist?
89. Name the dates which might be taken for the beginning of Mediaeval History.
90. Name the commanders and give the results of the following battles: Trasimenus, Zama, Phillippi and Actium.

Chapter XXX.—Mediaeval History Recreations.

I. RACES.

1. What event marks the beginning of Mediaeval History? Give the date of the Dawn and of Modern History.
2. Who were the Ostrogoths, Visigoths, Burgundians, Vandals, Merovingians, Lombards, Anglo-Saxons and Huns, and where did each race settle?
3. Explain why it was that the barbarians were converted to Christianity.
4. Define monasticism and tell why it flourished in the middle ages.
5. What were the Romance tongues?
6. When and what were the happenings under the reigns of Justinian and Heraclius?

II. Mohammedanism.

7. Who was Mohammed?
8. What was the Hegira?
9. What three things did the Mohammedans ask of other nations?
10. Describe the battle of Tours.
11. How was the empire divided?
12. State briefly the effects of Saracenic Civilization.

III. Crusades and Chivalry, etc.

13. Who were the crusaders, and why so called?
14. What was the general effect of the crusades?
15. Define Feudalism.
16. Define Chivalry.
17. Describe a castle.
18. How were the lands held?
19. State the order of procedure in conferring knighthood.
20. Describe the Tournament.
21. What effect had these practices upon the manners of the people?

IV. Rise of Modern Nations.

22. Who was Clovis, Pepin the Short, and Charlemagne?
23. What conquests did Charlemagne make, and how was his kingdom finally divided?
24. Where did the Northmen wander in the middle ages?
25. Who ruled France in the middle ages.
26. In whose reign did absolutism triumph?
27. Describe the battles of Crecy, Agincourt and Orleans, (briefly.)
28. When was the French Monarchy consolidated?
29. How many conquests were made of England? Give dates of each.
30. Tell of the conquest of Ireland, Wales and Scotland by England.
31. What events mark the growth of a constitutional monarchy in England?
32. Why was the War of the Roses so called? Give date.

33. What *great* names are connected with French and English Mediaeval History?
34. Compare the general condition of Germany with France and England.
35. Name and give dates of the different dynasties in Germany.
36. When was the "Great Interregnum?"
37. Describe the House of Hapsburg.
38. When did the Holy Roman Empire begin and end, and what was its condition in the Middle Ages?
39. When does Switzerland's History begin?
40. Name the three battles for Swiss Liberty.
41. What was the condition of her government?
42. Recite the legend of William Tell.
43. Describe the growth of the Papacy.
44. Who was the "last of the Tribunes?"
45. How did it happen that so many Italian cities became independent?
46. Name the chief of these cities, and tell something for which each is noted.
47. Give a brief sketch of Joan of Arc.
48. Who was John Huss? Sigismund? Maximilian?
49. Name some inventions of the Mediæval Period.
50. What was the condition of punishment in these times?
51. How many and what dates might be taken as the beginning of Modern History?
52. What inventions and happenings are clustered around these dates?
53. Who introduced printing into England?

Chapter XXXI.—Modern History Recreations.

I. Other Countries Than England.

1. What were the results of the wars of Charles VIII. of France?
2. Give results of the wars of Louis XII. in Italy.

3. What led to the Reformation?
4. Why were the reformers called Protestants?
5. What nations embraced the new doctrines?
6. What relation was Charles V. to Charles the Bold of Burgundy?
7. Name the rivals of Charles V.
8. Who was Loyola?
9. Give a sketch of the Guises.
10. Who was William the Silent?
11. What became of the different provinces of the Netherlands?
12. What became of William, Prince of Orange?
13. What noted descendant had he?
14. How were the Hapsburg dominions divided upon the death of Charles V?
15. Who was Solyman the magnificent?
16. Describe briefly the Turkish wars.
17. Describe the causes of the Thirty Years war.
18. Who was Wallenstein?
19. Who was Gustavus Adolphus?
20. What treaty closed the war?
21. What was accomplished by this war?
22. What countries made settlements in America?
23. Locate the principal or chief settlements of each country.
24. Why did Christina abdicate the throne of Sweden?
25. Who was Charles XII?
26. Give a sketch of the life of Peter the Great.
27. Tell of the dismemberment of Poland.
28. Who were the most influential Popes of Modern History?
29. Tell of Frederick the Great and the Rise of Prussia.
30. Describe the "War of the Austrian Succession."
31. Give a sketch of the reign of the Bourbons in France.
32. What was the policy of Cardinal Richilieu?
33. For what was Louis XIV. noted?
34. What followed Mazarin's death?

35. Give the causes and incidents (briefly) of the "War of the Spanish Succession?"
36. In what wars did Louis XIV. engage?
37. What possessions did France lose in the last war?
38. What led to the French Revolution?
39. What parties had they in this war?
40. Name some of the impetuous leaders of the French.
41. Name five generals of the Republic.
42. What dates mark the "Reign of Terror?"
43. What became of the royal family?
44. Give a sketch of Napoleon.
45. Who was Napoleon III?
46. Describe the Holy Alliance.
47. When did the Greek Revolution occur, and what was the result?
48. What Revolutions and wars occurred in 1848?
49. What was the seven years war? The seven weeks war? The seven months war?
50. Describe the Franco-Prussian war and give the results.
51. Mention all the chief recent modern events since this war.

II. ENGLAND.

52. What was done in England under the reign of Henry VIII.?
53. How many wives had he? Name them.
54. Describe his character.
55. Tell the story of Wolsley.
56. Who succeeded Henry VIII., and when?
57. Give a sketch of Somerset.
58. Who was lady Jane Grey?
59. Who was Mary Tudor.
60. Name the principal events of Queen Elizabeth's reign.
61. Give a sketch of Sir Walter Raleigh.
62. Describe the foreign policy of James I.
63. Of whom was it said, "He is the wisest fool in Europe?"
64. Who said it?

65. State the troubles between Charles I. and his parliament.
66. Who was Hampden? Strafford? Laud?
67. What parties had they in England then?
68. How long did the Civil War last.
69. What became of Charles I.?
70. Who succeeded him?
71. Give a sketch of Oliver Cromwell.
72. What bodies were called the Long and Short Parilaments?
73. When and what was the "Restoration?"
74. Describe the Gunpowder Plot.
75. What parties antedated the Cavaliers and Roundheads, and what parties have succeeded them?
76. When and under whose reign was the present Protestant version of the Bible translated?
77. Who were the "Pretenders?"
78. How did it happen that they were *only pretenders?*
79. Tell the story of the American Revolution.
80. Who succeeded Geo. IV.?
81. Describe the Crimean War.
82. Give a sketch of the British in India.
83. What was done by Warren Hastings, and who was he?
84. Who made the great speech against him?
85. Give a short sketch of the history of Australia.
86. What caused our second war with Great Britain?
87. Mention some recent events in English History.
88. Who is termed the "Grand Old Man?"
89. When did Queen Victoria come to the throne?
90. Who is the prime minister at present?
91. What did Cardinal Mazzini, the Italian patriot, say of the growth of liberty?

Chapter XXXII.—Answers to Questions on General History.

Ancient History—I. Egypt.

1. Egypt was founded by Menes about 3700 B. C.
2. The Hyksos or Shepherd Kings entered Egypt about 1900 B. C., and conquered the country, ruling it until 1525 B. C. The country prospered exceedingly under their reign. They were called the "Shepherd Kings" because they were herdsmen and brought their flocks with them.
3. Khufu and his successors. Rameses II.
4. Memphis and Thebes. Memphis was the first capital—founded by Menes, and supplanted by Thebes which arose in the Xth dynasty. (Thotmes III. was from Thebes.)
5. Persia, Greece, Rome, Turkey, France and England.
6. They were learned in the arts and sciences, but extremely superstitious and irreligious. They worshipped the gods Osiris, (husband), Isis, (wife) and Horus, (son), the planets, animals and the Nile river.
7. Pyramids, Obelisks, Sphinxes, Statues, Hieroglyphics and Mummies.

II. China and India.

8. Their policy of non-intercourse with other nations; reverence for their ancestors; the Great Wall; classics of Confucius; and memory cultivation.
9. They consider it a disgrace for a child to learn more than his parents knew, and they had four kinds of religion. In China, Confucianism or a following after the teachings of Confucius, Taoism or a system of reasoning, were both followed; while in India Brahmanism, as taught by the priest Brahma, was followed, and Buddhism, as presented by Buddha, is practiced in both countries.
10. (a) He was the greatest teacher of China and flourished

in the 5th century B. C. (b) Chewang-te built the great wall (215—204 B. C.)
11. China, 3000 B. C.   India, 1500 B. C.
12. They regarded them as barbarians.

III. BABYLONIA-ASSYRIA.

13. Assyria, 1250 B. C.   Babylonia, 625 B. C.
14. Tiglathinin.
15. Babylon was founded by Nimrod, a mighty hunter, about 4000 B. C.
16. Babylon was noted for her monuments, hanging gardens and aquariums. She was five times as large as London is now, and the admiration of the then known world.
17. Nabopolassar, Nebuchednezzar and Belshazzar.
18. Babylon, which was the seat of government until 1250 B. C., and rose again 625 B. C., and Nineveh, which was the capital from 1256 B. C. to 625 B. C.
19. Belshazzar, the last King of Babylon, held a great feast and amid the uproar of drunken revelry, a hand was seen writing on the wall in his room. The King was much astonished and sent for his astrologers and soothsayers, but none of them could explain the meaning of the words:—"Mene-mene-Tekel-Upharsin"—which were written. At last the King sent for Daniel and he interpreted it as follows: "The days of thy kingdom are numbered. Thou art weighed in the balance and found wanting, and thy kingdom shall be divided among the Persians." That very night Cyrus turns the Euphrates from its course, enters the city and captures it.

IV. PHOENICIA AND JUDEA.

20. They invented the alphabet, and were noted as commercial people and traders.
21. About 1550 B. C.
22. Sidon and Tyre.
23. Carthage was founded in Africa on the Mediterranean

sea by Phoenicians from Tyre in 880 B. C.
24. The beginning of the Patriarchal Age, 2000 B. C.
25. The Exodus was the *going out* or the removal of the Israelites from Egypt. It occurred in 1491 B. C.
26. Saul, David and Solomon.
27. The division occurred in 975 B. C. and two of the tribes known as *Judah* accepted Rehoboam as their King, and had their capital at Jerusalem; and the other ten tribes known as *Israel* made Jeroboam King with their capital at Samaria. These last tribes were captured by Sargon and finally became known as the "lost tribes."
28. They are scattered over the face of the earth, being the most numerous in Russia and Austro-Hungary.

V. MEDO-PERSIA.

29. The Medes under Cyaxares were the leading nation at first, overthrowing Nineveh. Astyges, the son of Cyaxares, became the father-in-law of Cyrus of Persia, and Cyrus attended the King's court so much that he was liked by the Medis who revolted and were united into one nation under Cyrus with the Persians.
30. Cyrus, who captured Babylon (Darius of the Bible).
31. The Medes and Persians seldom, if ever, changed their minds in regard to either laws or customs. See Daniel VI—12.
32. It was as extravagant as the modern one of Louis XIV., but not so profligate. Wines were freely used. The King had upwards of fifteen thousand servants and attendants, besides numerous courtiers, and spies of every description, imaginable, almost.
33. Cyrus, Cambyses and Darius I.
34. 538 B. C.; 500 B. C.; 486 B. C. on until 330 B. C., when it becomes subject to Greece.
35. Zoroastrianism, which was the worship of Zoroaster as taught in the book, "Zend-avesta." It taught a system of dualism in nature, Ormazd being the God

of Light, and Ahrimann, the God of Darkness. They worshipped both of these Gods; Magianism, or the worship of the magicians; and the Ghebers or worshippers of fire.

VI. GREECE.

36. The Pelasgians, who were conquered and absorbed by the Hellenes.
37. Paris, the son of Priam, King of Troy, had seized Helen, wife of Menelaus, King of Sparta, and carried her off to his home. Agamemnon, the brother-in-law of Menelaus, together with a lot of Grecian warriors sails for Troy to avenge the wrong. They laid siege to Troy for nine years and finally took the city by the statagem of the wooden horse. Achilles, Ajax, Ulysses, Nestor and Diomed were chiefs in this mythological war.
38. The Dorians and Ionians were the races of early Greece, and the Spartans and Athenians were the leading classes of later Greece.
39. Lycurgus of Sparta. Draco and Solon of Athens.
40. A tyrant, formerly, meant one who usurped power, and he might be either a good or a bad ruler. The word slave, simply meant a servant.
41. The word is derived from the Greek word *ostros*, a shell. When the people disliked a statesman, or general, they wrote his name on shells, and if a majority of the shells were written (i. e. with the name on them) on, the man whose name was so inscribed was banished for life, or for a stated period, from his country.
42. In 490 B. C. at Marathon, between the Greeks under Miltiades, and the Persians under Datis and Artaphernes. The Greeks won a signal victory.
43. (a) Xerxes, King of Persia, who had 1,500,000 men. (b) At the pass of Thermopylae. (c) At Salamis, on water, and at Platea and Mycale on land, 479 B. C.

44. A noted ruler under the Athenian Leadership (479 B. C. to 431 B. C.)
45. The protection afforded by her walls and Persian gold.
46. The retreat of 10,000 Greeks under Xenophon who made a foolhardy expedition against Cyrus, the Younger of Persia.
47. Alexander the Great. He was the son of Philip of Macedonia, who already had all of the other Grecian states at his feet. Alexander became King when he was only twenty years old, (335 B. C.) and after he had dealt some of his crushing blows upon his rebellious subjects, he entered upon a world-conquering tour. He crossed the Hellespont with 35,000 men and in the decisive battles of Granicus, Issus and Arbela he defeated the Persians and took possession of their empire. He next conquered India, and was preparing to attack Carthage and Sicily when a sudden fever put an end to his military career. He died at the age of 32, having reigned thirteen years.
48. There was much contention among his generals for many years, but after the battle of Ipsus, 301 B. C., it was divided as follows: Seleucus received Syria and the East; Lysimachus, Thrace and Asia Minor; Ptolemy, Egypt, and Cassander, Greece and Macedonia.
49. In 30 B. C.
50. The Spartans were taught to be adroit, skillful and cultivated bluntness. Their training was of a military nature. The Athenians were taught manners, rhythms, and harmonies and gymnastics. They cultivated a taste for the beautiful in nature and art.
51. Thucydides, Diodorus-Siculus, Herodotus and Plutarch. (Answers may differ on these questions as found in this book.)
52. Homer, Hesiod, Pindar and Aeschylus.
53. (a) The immortal Demosthenes, Pericles, Aeschines and Anaxagoras. (b) Zeuxis, Apollodonis, Parrha-

sius and Melanthius. (c) Phidias, Polyclitus, Myron and Praxiteles.
54. See page 28. Dates are 550 B. C., 350 B. C., 330 B. C., and 475 B. C. respectively.
55. *Bravery.*
56. Sparta and Athens, and Thebes and Corinth.
57. Miltiades, Themistocles, Aristides, Alcibiades, Epaminondas, Agesilaus II., Philip and Alexander the Great.
58. They worshipped great imaginary gods, and about three thousand minor gods and goddesses. (See outline on Greece.) It was purely a mythological religion.
59. The Turks were trying to revolutionize the world and they took Constantinople in 1453 A. D. Greece revolted in the 19th century and became free by the assistance of England and France.
60. A Grecian leader in the war for independence against Turkey. He was killed at the battle of Missolonghi.
61. This battle was fought in 1824. The Greeks were successful, although their leader was killed.

VII. ROME.

62. It was founded by Romulus in 753 B. C.
63. The Patricians or nobles, and the Plebeians or common people.
64. (a) Cincinnatus was a plowman, who was waited upon by a committee from the Senate which informed him that he was chosen to lead the armies of Rome and save his country. He did their bidding and saved his country, but could not be persuaded to remain at the head of affairs of State and went back to his plow. (c) Horatio, single-handed, held a bridge and kept the Etruscans at bay until the Romans had a chance to save themselves by swimming the Tiber.
65. He was one of the first consuls under the Republic in 509 B. C., and he sentenced two of his own sons to death for being traitors. He was killed in a battle

with the Etruscans, but the Romans were victorious.
66. Seven.
67. Romulus, Numa Pompilius, Tullius Hostilius, Ancus Martius, Tarquin the Elder, Servius Tullius and Tarquin the Proud.
68. Hannibal. He was successful for a number of years, but was finally overcome by the odds against him.
69. When the Jugurthine war occurred, (110-109 B. C.) Marius was made consul, and Sulla, a bright but dissolute young man, was general. The general was to obey the consul, and the consul could not serve for a period longer than two years. They both violated these laws, and torn by internal strife, and harrassed by the barbarians, Rome entered into a civil war. At first Marius was expelled, and Sulla with his conquering legions captured Rome. Then Marius gathered a force of troops and he came back and took the imperial city, but died (88 B. C.) before Sulla returned from his conquering tour in Asia. Next followed a reign of terror for Sulla murdered 6,000 soldiers of the opposite party. After three years of dreadful rule he resigned suddenly, and died (78 B. C). (b) Cataline was a dissolute nobleman who secretly attempted (63 B. C.) to overthrow the Roman government by assassinating the consuls. The plot seemed likely to succeed, until Cicero, the orator and lawyer, became acquainted with the facts, when prompt measures were introduced to stop it. Cataline died leading his rebellious citizens and Cicero, for his work, has been hailed as the "Father of His Country."
70. Cæsar, Pompey and Crassus; 60 B. C.
71. The other two got the wealth of Crassus, who was murdered while fighting in Parthia. Pompey and Cæsar acted in harmony for a time, but jealousies arose and Cæsar defeated Pompey gaining the throne.

72. Octavius, (Augustus) Antony and Lepidus. 31 B. C.
73. Lepidus was weak minded and soon disposed of by the others. Antony held out against his superiors, until the charms of the Egyptian Cleopatra subdued him, and Augustus or Octavius becomes another, if not a greater "Cæsar."
74. He was defeated at Actium in 31 B. C., and again at Alexandria where he killed himself.
75. 30 B. C.
76. Jesus who is called Christ. He was born when Augustus was emperor.
77. Caligula, one of the emperors.
78. Nero.
79. Nerva, Trajan, Hadrian and the two Antonines.
80. In 260 A. D., upon the death of Valerian, King of Rome, various fragments of the empire set up petty governments whose chiefs were known as the "Thirty Tyrants."
81. Constantine who had always been friendly to the Christians was marching into Italy with his army in 312 A. D., when he saw a light, and a flaming cross in the sky with the inscription on it, "In Hoc Signo Vinces" (By this sign conquer). He adopted the emblem, and was converted to Christianity."
82. Just after the death of Theodosius in 395 A. D.
83. Alaric, Attila and Genseric.
84. Romulus Augustulus, 476 A. D.
85. (a) Plautus, Virgil, Horace and Ovid. (b) Cicero, Seneca and the two Plinys. (c) Cato the Censor, Cæsar, Sallust and Livy.
86. These combats were advertised by public announcements, and on the day or the exhibition, decorations were profuse. Syrian perfumes were laden on the air and the gladiators, marched into the arena in pairs to the sweetest strains of music. When one was severely wounded by a lance or spear (or was thrown from his horse) he held up his forefinger as

a plea for life. A waving of the handkerchief meant mercy, and the extended thumb and clinched fist forbade hope.

87. 1. Babylonia-Assyrian. 2. Persian. 3. Grecian. 4. Roman. 5. Mohammedan. 6. Charlemagne's.
88. A study of the Greek and Latin authorities, Mythology, Architecture and Agriculture.—It was a *classical* education.
89. 1. Alaric in Rome, 410 B. C.—2. Battle of Chalons 451 B. C.—3. Downfall of Rome, 476 A. D.
90.

BATTLES.	GENERALS.	PARTIES AND RESULTS.	DATE.
1. Trasimenus.	Flaminius............ Hannibal.............	Romans defeated by Carthaginians............	B. C. 217
2. Zama	Scipio Africanus....... Hannibal.............	Romans Victorious	201
3. Phillipi........	Brutus and Cassius....... Octavius and Antony...	Brutus and Cassius defeated........	42
4. Actium	Antony and Cleopatra. Octavius.............	Octavius victorious.............	31

Chapter XXXIII.—Mediaeval History.

I. RACES.

1. The downfall of Rome, 476 A. D.; 1100 A. D.; 1500 A. D.
2. (a) The ostrogoths were a powerful barbaric tribe in the east of Germany. (b) The Visigoths were in Western Germany. They were related to each other. (c) The Burgundians came from the north-east and settled in Central Europe. (d) The Vandals were a devastating tribe of Northern Africa. (e) The Merovingians were a weak Northern Germanic tribe. (f) The Lombards were from the East, and so called because of their long beards. They settled in Lombardy. (g) The Huns, after securing all Europe finally settled (some of them) in Hungary. (h) The Anglo-Saxons were descendants of the

Goths, and named from the sections in which they had settled. They settled and named Angle-land or England.
3. While they were carrying destruction with their arms wherever they went, they met the plain, common, humble followers of Christ, whose examples of piety touched the tender hearts of the barbarians; and the countries conquered with the sword, generally, conquered the conquerors with their *religion*.
4. The word is derived from the Greek, *monacho*, meaning a monk. It was the practice of the Catholic Church, of having monks assemble in groups or monasteries, for the purpose of spiritual education. By this means alone was the Bible, and all records of Christianity saved and promulgated. It flourished, therefore, because it was deemed a necessity.
5. The barbaric languages which were Romanized or Latinized. Such as the Italian, French and Spanish.
6. Under the reign of Justinian, the Emperor of the East occurred: (1) The adornment of his capital; (2) the writing of the Pandects, Codes and Institutes of Roman Law; (3) and the defeat of the Goths in Italy by his general, Belisarius. While Heraclius was on the throne was fought the battle of Nineveh (627 A. D.) and Persia was overthrown.

II. MOHAMMEDANISM.

7. He was an Arabian camel driver and was born in Mecca in 571 A. D. He called himself God's prophet and founded a new religion.
8. The *flight* of Mohammed from his place of nativity to Medina in 622 A. D. was called "Hegira."
9. The "Koran," tribute or the sword. Other nations must either accept their doctrines, pay them tribute or be put to death.
10. The Mohammedans had been successful in their world-conquering expedition, and marched northward from Spain. Here they met the Franks under Charles

Martel ("The Hammer") in 732 A. D. After a fierce and spirited battle in which 375,000 men were left dead on the field, the Mohammedans or Saracens met their first defeat, and the Pyrenees became the northern boundary of the Saracenic Empire in Europe.

11. The "Ommiades" held Spain with their capital at Cordova; the "Abassides" ruled Northern Africa and Arabia from their capital at Bagdad; and the descendants of Ali, son-in-law of Mohammed, controlled Persia, Egypt and Mauretania.

12. At the time of the introduction of Mohammedanism, the other religions were almost lifeless, and the Christian Church, especially, was very weak. This accounts for their wonderful influence. They established schools at Cordova and Bagdad, and as all Europe was buried beneath the flood of ignorance, people from all parts of the world had to resort to these schools for education. They gave us Algebra, Arithmetic, and many other commendable things.

III. CRUSADES, CHIVALRY, ETC.

13. They were those Christians who desired to rescue the Holy Land of Palestine and the Tomb of Christ from the Moslems or Mohammedans. They used the cross as their emblem, hence they were called Croisaders or Crusaders, (i. e. followers of the Cross.)

14. Although the general effect was entirely different from the object in view, yet it was beneficial to Europe. 1. The minds of Crusaders were enlightened by contact with customs, different from their own. 2. They introduced, into Europe, sugar, silk and fine wheat from the East. 3. Principalities, duchies and counties warred with each other after the crusading ceased. 4. The Church's power increased. 5. The Crusades brought chivalry. 6. A rivalry arose between Italian free cities in regard to the Eastern

trade. 7. Secret societies were fostered and encouraged.

15. Feudalism was that system by means of which knights and lords held their lands on condition of military service to the King, or chief, who granted them, and they in turn held vassals under them upon the same condition.

15. Chivalry was a training of skilled knights from boyhood. At the age of seven years, the boy became a Page and had certain duties to perform. When he was fourteen years old he became a Squire, and at 21 he was knighted if he had stood all the previous tests and performed the strict duties exacted of him.

17. It was usually a strong stone fortress on some high cliff inclosed by massive parapetted walls, encircled by ditches shining with towers.

18. The lands were held by the people at the will of their lords, vassals, fiefs or suzerains upon condition of service to them.

19. The candidate on bended knees took a vow to defend his lord's good name and to be his (lord's) man, to not shun any adventure in any war he might happen to be, and to protect women and all weak persons. He was then stricken on the neck with the flat side of the sword and dubbed a knight.

20. Lists were painted and gilded and hung with gorgeous tapestries. The combatants (knights clad in armor on horseback) appeared at the sound of music, and rushed towards each other with frantic fury. They were sometimes preceded by ladies who led them with golden chains. There were knights and heralds posted at places in the lists to replace broken lances and weapons, and to assist or raise unhorsed knights, and see that order was observed.

21. The effect of chivalry was to cause people to be more

polite, to make them respect weakness, and honor women.

IV. Rise of Modern Nations.

22. (a) King of the Franks from 487-507 A. D. (b) Pepin, the Short, was the son of Charles Martel and King of the Franks. (c) Charlemagne was the son of Pepin, conqueror of Italy and Germany, and Emperor of the Holy Roman Empire from 800-814 A. D.
23. He conquered all that territory from the Baltic to the Adriatic Sea, and from the English channel to the East of Burgundy, and re-established the Holy Roman Empire.—800. At the Treaty of Verdun in 843 A. D. Lothair obtained Italy, Louis held Germany and the Rhine, and Charles the Bold, France. All these were his grand sons.
24. They went to Normandy in France, Russia, Greenland and Iceland.
25. The Merovingian, Carlovingian, Capetian and Valois families.
26. In the reign of Louis XI.—1461-1483.
27. a. Crecy was fought between the English, under Edward III., and the French, under Philip VI., in France in 1346. The French were defeated. b. Henry V. of England defeated an army of French four times as large as his own, at Agincourt in 1415. The French were commanded by Charles VI. c. The English had laid siege to Orleans in 1429, but Joan of Arc, a simple, peasant girl who believed she was inspired of heaven to save her country, appeared at the head of the French army and the English retreated.
28. Under Charles VII., aided by Joan of Arc in 1422.
29. 1. Roman Conquest—79 A. D. 2. Saxon Conquest—about 400 A. D. 3. The Danish Conquest—1016 A. D. 4. Norman Conquest—1066 A. D.
30. a. Ireland was conquered by the barons of Henry II., 1154-1189, but rebelled and defeated the Earl of Es-

sex in 1589, and was again beaten by Ireton, son-in-law of Oliver Cromwell, in 1651. b. Wales was subdued by Edward I. in 1300 A. D. His son, Edward II., attempted to conquer Scotland, but such men as Wallace and Bruce proved too much for him and he was defeated. c. The Crowns were united under the monarch, James VI. of Scotland, who became James I. of England, in 1603.—Union of Parliament later.

31. 1. The war of the barons against King John, in 1215, and the obtainment of the "Great Charter." 2. The war of Parliament against the King, Charles I., led by Oliver Cromwell—1644-48. 3. The rise of the House of Commons from 1640 since. 4. The Granting of the Petition of Right—1628. 4. Bill of Rights—1689.

32. Two ladies, discussing the troubles between the Houses of York and Lancaster, exhibited White and Red Roses, respectively, to exemplify the purity of the one and the beauty of the other. It began in 1455 and lasted for thirty years.

33. 1. Charlemagne. 2. Joan of Arc. 3. Hugh Capet. Louis XI. 5. Richard I. 6. Alcuin. See p. 52.

34. France and England were almost continually at war with each other, while Germany struggled against the Barbarians in order to hold the title of "Emperor of the Holy Roman Empire," established by Charlemagne in 800.

35. Carlovingians, Franconians, Saxons, Hohenstaufens and Hapsburgs. (See outlines for dates.)

36. From 1253 until 1273.

37. It was named from Rudolph's Castle in Switzerland, and was proud, haughty and revengeful.

38. It lasted until 1807. (See Ans. to No. 34.) It was an empty honor, confered on the weak rulers of Germany, in the middle ages.

39. In 1307, when a little band met and swore that they would have liberty.
40. Morgarten—1315. Sempach—1386. Nafels—1388.
41. Her independence was acknowledged in 1648. The country at first comprised only eight cantons, or districts, but it now has 22 cantons. It became a republic, and such a one that no nation dared to tread upon its rights.
42. William Tell was put in prison and his son was arrested. Gessler, the Austrian governor, told Tell if he would shoot an apple off his son's head, at the distance of 100 paces, he (Gessler) would grant them both liberty. Tell was very skillful with the bow, but he hid an arrow in his vest that he might shoot Gessler, should he hit his boy. Tell hits the apple, but Gessler, discovering the hidden arrow, put him in prison again. One time after this, they were in a boat on a stormy lake, and Tell's chains were unloosen that he might steer the boat, when he jumped out od a rock, hid and shot Gessler, killing him.
43. The monasteries kept alive the lights of learning, because they were peaceful, did acts of devotion, furnished homes for the oppressed, practiced benevolence, and restrained feudalism when it was too much for even the Kings. The gift of Pepin, the Short, made the pope a political prince; the crusades strengthened the papal power; and the belief that the world would come to an end in 1000 A. D. all increased the power of the Papacy.
44. Rienzi, the Roman Patriot.
45. When the Roman Empire was destroyed, it began to crumble, and the strongest cities had to prepare for a struggle for existence against the barbarians.
46. Florence, the birthplace of Amerigo Vespucci; Genoa, the birthplace of Columbus; Venice, built on seventy-two small islands.
47. She was the daughter of a peasant and believed that

God had inspired her to save the French. Leaving home, she entered the army and led it to victory against the English. She had the Dauphin crowned King of Rheims, and declared that her mission was ended; but the silly King insisted that she must remain with the army. She was captured by the English, and burned at the stake in 1431 at the age of 20. She foretold, amid the flames, that the English would soon meet with disasters.

48. a. A protestant reformer of Bohemia. b. Emperor of Hungary and Bohemia. c. Emperor of Germany before the Reformation.
49. The inventions of gunpowder, printing and the mariner's compass. (See tables for authors, &c.)
50. They were extremely severe. Heretics were burned at the stake, which was the punishment for severe crimes, and was always administered by almost all religious denominations and rulers.
51. 1. 1453—Close of the "Hundred Years War." 2. Downfall of Constantinople. 3. 1491—Expulsion of the Moors from Spain. 4. 1492—Discovery of America. 5. 1500—As a general date including all these events.
52. Deliverance of France; War of the Roses; Conquest of Granada; Printing of first book by Gutenburg; The Tudor family comes to the throne of England; Vasco DeGama doubles the Cape of Good Hope; Savonarola is burned at the stake; Charles VIII. invaded Italy; and Chivalry becomes obsolete.
53. William Caxton.

Chapter XXXIV.—Modern History.

II. Other Countries than England.

1. They gave the French a thirst for conquest for which Italy suffered often, and led to acquaintances which

resulted in Philip, heir to the Netherlands, marrying Joanna, daughter of Ferdinand and Isabella, while Catharine, Joanna's sister, married Arthur of England, and became heir to the British crown, upon the death of Henry, brother of Arthur.
2. He was at first successful, but committed such brutal outrages, and his best general Gaston de Foix having been killed at Ravenna in 1512, he was defeated.
3. Wealth and undisputed power had probably led the church into some abuses, and some men thought and felt that the Popes were not true representatives of Christ.
4. The Diet of the Church at Spires, 1529, declared that no changes from the doctrines and worship would be allowed, and the German princes and cities that *protested* against this were termed Protestants.
5. Denmark, Sweden and a part of Germany and Switzerland, the Netherlands and England.
6. He was the great grand-son of Charles the Bold of Burgundy.
7. See p. 57.
8. Ignatius Loyola was a Spanish cavalier, who had once been wounded in battle. He led a counter-influence for the Catholic church against Luther by founding the grand order of *Jesuits*.
9. The Guises were descended from the Dukes of Lorraine. Mary married James V. of Scotland, and her daughter, Mary, married Francis II. of France. Hence they had a wonderful influence, at the Scottish and French courts, against the English. The Duke of Guise defended Metz against Charles V. who had an army of 100,000 men, and he captured Calais. He has been accused of being the chief promoter of the massacre of St. Bartholomew—1572, and he seized Paris itself at one time. Henry, the heir to the French crown, invited him to a conference and had him stabbed to death.

10. William, Prince of Orange, in the Netherlands.
11. In the war for the "Rise of the Dutch Republic," William attempted to unite them all together but failed. The Ten lower provinces were however united to the seven upper ones in 1814.
12. He was murdered in his own house by a hired assassin of Philip II., of Spain in 1584.
13. His grandson, William, who married Mary, daughter of James II., of England, and headed the Revolution of 1688, winning the English crown.
14. His brother, Ferdinand, became emperor of Germany and Duke of Austria; and Philip obtained Spain and the Netherlands, yet they acted in concert.
15. He was the ruler of Turkey and the great Mohammedan leader of Modern Times.
16. Solyman had captured Cypress and alarmed all Europe. The Spanish and Venetians succeeded in defeating the Turks in the battle of Lepanto, 1571. Solyman's death caused a lull in the wars as his immediate successor, Selim, was a weak monarch; but when Mohammed II. had murdered his nineteen brothers in order to gain the throne, he, of course, renewed the war, and at Kerestes, in 1596, 50,000 Christians were slain. They, the Mohammedans, were, however, beaten, and Bohemia and Hungary were relieved from paying them tribute.
17. The crowns of Bohemia and Hungary were resigned to Ferdinand of Styria. The Bohemians revolted against Ferdinand and chose Frederick the Palatinate, and son-in-law of James I. of England, as their king. See p. 61.
18. He was the Imperial general and leader of the Catholic forces and was never defeated until he met Gustavus Adolphus. He was assassinated under orders of the emperor for treason,
19. He was the Protestant King of Sweden, who led his troops to victory against the famous Wallenstein at

Lutzen in 1632. He died amid the victorious shouts of his soldiers.
20. The Treaty of Westphalia in 1648.
21. 1. It brought the religious wars on the continent to an end; 2. granted religious freedom; 3. recognized the independence of Switzerland; 4. and Holland; 5. and gave Alsace to France; 6. and Pomerania to Sweden. The causes were forgotten.
22. Spain, Portugal, England, France, Holland and Sweden.
23. 1. The Spaniards settled in Mexico, S. A., Cuba, Hayti and the Phillipines; 2. The Portuguese in Brazil and various islands; 3. The English in Virginia, Mass., N. H., Conn., R. I., N. C. and S. C., Georgia and Guiana; 4. The Dutch in New York, Guiana, Java and Spice Islands; 5. The French in Canada, Guiana and La.; 6. The Swedes in Delaware.
24. She was only six years old when Gustavus Adolphus her father was killed. She displayed remarkable ability, but no steadiness of purpose, and became tired of governing, so she resigned in favor of her cousin Charles X., and spent the rest of her life in aimless wandering.
25. Charles XII. of Sweden was a grandson of Charles X. He came to the throne in 1697, at fifteen years of age. His enemies attempted to take advantage of his youth and divide his kingdom, but in two weeks he defeated the King of Denmark. Russia had besieged Narva with 80,000 men, and he went to its relief with only 8,000 Swedes and beat *them*. Next he crushed Poland, placing Stanislaus Leczinksy on the throne, and driving Augustus the Strong into Saxony. Imagining himself a second Alexander he invaded Russia, but was defeated at Pultowa in 1709, and killed in a siege in Norway before he reached home in 1718.
26. He became joint-king with his demented half-brother, when he was ten years old. At the age of seventeen

he siezed the crown for himself—1689. He went to England, Holland and other countries and learned the art of ship-building, and observed everything that could be of any use to his country. He desired an outlet on the Baltic sea, and entered into a coalition with Poland and Denmark, to dismember Sweden. Charles XII. was more than successful against Peter at first, but the Russians learned lessons from his defeats, and finally succeeded in routing the Swedes at Pultowa, and raised Russia from a fourth rate to first rate power. He died in 1725, and was succeeded by his wife, Catherine I.

27. Catherine II. of Russia attempts to secure Poland, but Austria and Prussia interfered and they agreed to divide it into thirds. This was done in 1772. The Poles under Kosciusko struggled fiercely but were beaten by overwhelming odds, and the most disgraceful act ever perpetrated in the annals of history was committed by the greedy trio.

28. Leo X., Gregory XIII. and Pius IX.

29. His grand-father, the elector of Brandenburg was humored by the Emperor, and crowned as King of Prussia. Frederick the Great came to the throne in 1740, and having an inherent genius for war, he entered the "War of the Austrian Succession," and the "Seven Years War"—1756-63, and by so doing he placed Prussia among the leading powers of Europe.

30. In 1740, Maria Theresa became heir to the Austrian throne by the "Pragmatic Sanction" arranged by her father, but other claims caused Prussia, France and Spain to war against Great Britain and Holland. The treaty of Aix-la-Chapelle in 1748 closed the war and left Frederick in possession of Silesia.

31. Henry of Navarre, as Henry IV., was the first Bourbon. Louis XVI. the last one in successive order, was beheaded in 1793. Louis XVIII. "tackled" the

throne two or three times, but Napoleon I. interfered with his regal robes, as did Napoleon III. with another Kingdom. The Last Bourbon on the throne was Charles X.—1824-30. The Bourbons like the Stuarts of England, believed in the "Divine Right of Kings" and were obstinate and cruel at times. The Revolution of 1830 placed Louis Phillippe on the throne and since that time no Bourbon has applied for the situation.

32. He had three things to accomplish, viz: to destroy the Huguenots; subdue the nobles; and humble the House of Hapsburg or Austria. Under his regime, Louis XIII. became the "first man in Europe." though he was only the "second man in France."
33. He was noted for his false ideas of glory, his independence of ministers and reckless extravagance.
34. Louis XIV. became his own prime minister, and was sole master of France for fifty years.
35. The King of Spain, Charles II., had willed his dominions to the grandson of Louis XIV., who accepted the crown in his (grand-son's) behalf. Other countries feared that the union of two such powerful nations would endanger Europe, so England, Holland and Austria formed a Grand Alliance to prevent it. They espoused the cause of Archduke Charles of Austria, but in the midst of the war, he became Emperor of Germany, so now they feared *one* as much as the *other*. The Treaties of Utrecht and Rastadt in 1714 closed the war, after twelve years of fighting by which nothing was gained or lost in principle.
36. See p. 62.
37. She lost Nova Scotia, Newfoundland and Hudson's Bay in America, and all she had claimed of the Spanish Netherlands.
38. See p. 67.
39. Jacobins, Cordeliers, Girondists, Royalists and Terrorists.

40. Danton, Marat and Robespierre.
41. Pichegru, Hoche, Jourdan, Moreau and Dumouriez.
42. That period from June 2, 1793 to July 28, 1794.
43. The Queen fled to England, but the little son Louis XVII. died after two years suffering in prison. Romance has pictured him as coming to America.
44. He was born on the island of Corsica in 1769, and attended a military school at Brienne, in France, when he was only ten years old, He was resolute, quarrelsome and gloomy, but proud, a genius and a favorite with his teachers. He entered the army as a lieutenant and first distinguished himself at the siege of Toulon. He married Josephine, widow of Beauharnais, who was executed, and obtained command of the army of Italy in 1796. He was successful in this campaign and afterwards defeated Austria. All Europe soon trembled at his power, for monarchies crumbled and Kings tumbled at his command. Victories succeeded each other, thick and fast, until all Europe met him at Leipsic in 1813, where he was defeated and banished to the island of Elba. He escaped the guards, and in one hundred days from the time of his banishment, was back again, and met the allied armies under Wellington at Waterloo in 1815, but was beaten only because his marshal Grouchy failed to appear on the scene of action. He was again banished to an island—St. Helena—where he died in 1821. Had he not made some flagrant mistakes, the map of Europe might today present different boundary lines to our vision.
45. He was a nephew of Napoleon I. and by means of a revolution, he became the chief officer of the second republic, which being changed to a monarchy made him King—1848-71.
46. Alexander I., Czar of Russia, proposed to the five great powers of Russia, Austria, Prussia, France and Great Britain that they "Remain united in true broth-

erly love; govern their subjects as parents; and maintain religion, peace and justice." This was nice, but a spirit of Liberalism as opposed to Absolutism, under despotic monarchs, arose and led to the revolutions of 1848.

47. It occurred in 1823 and lasted until 1830. The Greeks became independent of Turkey, and a Prince of Denmark was placed on the throne.

48. 1. The Italians rebel against Austria. 2. The Hungarians led by Kossuth revolt. 3. The Duchies of of Schleswig and Holstein rebel against Denmark. 4. The Revolution in France. 5. The Chartists in England. 6. The Revolution in Germany.

49. a. The war of Austria, with France, Russia, Saxony, Sweden and Poland as allies against Prussia to recover Silesia. England alone aided Prussia.—1756–1763. b. It was Prussia and Italy against Austria, this time, and Austria was defeated and shut out of the German Empire.—1866. c. The war of Prussia and other German states against France in 1870–1871, in which France was defeated, and the King of Prussia became Emperor of Germany.

50. France desired to perpetuate German divisions, and Napoleon III. imagined himself a second *Bonaparte*, and the French shouted "on to Berlin." The Battles of Weissenburg, Worth, Courcelles, Thionville and Gravelotte were all German victories, and Napoleon surrendered 80,000 men at Sedan, and his general, Marshal Bazaine, 180,000 at Mitz. Thus France, which held Europe in awe, under one Napoleon for 197 months, lay at the mercy of one nation under another Napoleon, in seven months.

51. 1. The Pope ceases to be a temporal prince, because the states of the Church were added to Italy.—1878. 2. Turkey grants religious toleration in 1878. 3. Wilhelmina, the child queen, succeeds her father William III. as ruler of the Netherlands.—1890.

4. *Alexander II. of Russia is assassinated in 1881.
5. The Edict of 1890 against the Jews. 6. The Famine of 1890-92. 7. Japan becomes a Constitutional Monarchy.—1889. 8. China and Japan war with each other.—1895. 9. The Russo-Turkish war of 1878. 10. The Graeco-Turkish War of 1897. 11. Italian and Abyssinian affairs.—1897. 12. Rebellion of Cuba and Philipines.—1897-1898. 13. War between United States and Spain.—1898. 14. Death of Hon. W. E. Gladstone.—1898. 15. European intervention in the Orient.—1898. 16. Dewey's victory at Manila.—1898.

II. ENGLAND.

52. The wars with Francis I. and Charles V. The breach with the Catholic Church, and domestic troubles.
53. See p. 60.
54. He was full of whims, obstinate and extremely cruel and ungenerous.
55. Cardinal Wolsley, his prime minister, was authorized to procure a divorce for him from Catharine—No. 1—so he could marry Anne Boleyn, but the King, suspecting his fidelity, because the matter was delayed, had him arrested for treason. He died while on his way to prison, broken-hearted.
56. Edward VI. in 1547.
57. The Duke of Somerset became regent for Edward VI., who was only ten years old. The Duke of Northumberland an arch-enemy to Somerset persuaded the King to have him executed and set aside his half-sisters, Mary and Elizabeth, and let *his* cousin receive the crown.
58. This cousin, see 57, to the Duke was Lady Jane Grey, a beautiful and accomplished girl, who was proclaimed Queen against her wishes, and she and Lord Dudley, her husband were imprisoned and executed for treason.

*The same year Garfield was assassinated.

59. She was the daughter of Henry VIII. and Catharine of Aragon, and married her cousin, Philip II. of Spain.
60. 1. The defeat of the Invincible Armada—1588. 2. The Independence of Holland. 3. Re-establishment of Protestantism. 4. Increase of Commerce. 5. Her numerous Favorites. 6. The "Augustan Age" of Literature for the English. 7. Drake sails around the Globe. 8. Hawkins traces the coast of Guinea. 9. Formation of the East India Company. 10. Colonization attempted by Raleigh in Va.
61. He was one of Queen Elizabeth's favorites, and made the first attempt to colonize Virginia. He introduced smoking into England, and potatoes into Ireland. He seems to have incurred the displeasure of the Sovereign, and was imprisoned for thirteen years, during which time he wrote a "History of the World." King James I. released him and sent him to S. A. for gold, but Raleigh found none, so he was vexed, and had him beheaded.
62. It was weak and effeminate. He courted favors of Spain, refused to help his son-in-law, the Elector-Palatine of Germany, when England clamored for war, and Great Britain for a period ceased to be the leading nation on the continent.
63. This was said of James I. of England.
64. Sully, the great French statesman.
65. The King attempted to establish absolutism as it was in France, and in 1628 Parliament wrested from him the Petition of Right, which curtailed the sovereign's power. Charles disregarded all his promises and for eleven years ruled like Louis XI. No parliament had been convoked, and when the Scotch invaded England the King had to succumb and call a parliament. This was his "Waterloo," for the parliament brought his famous advisers to the block, and even the proud Charles himself mounted the scaffold in 1649.

66. [a.] Hampden was the first parliamentarian general and a cousin to Oliver Cromwell. [b.] Stafford and Laud were advisers of Charles I., and were executed by parliament for their cruel punishments.
67. The adherents of the King's cause were called *cavaliers*, and those who advocated the cause of Parliament were called *Roundheads*..
68. Four years—1642-48.
69. He was beheaded in 1649, as a result of his defeat by parliament.
70. Oliver Cromwell who was styled the Protectorate of the Commonwealth.
71. He belonged to that sturdy independent party of the Puritans or Roundheads, and trained his army after his own plan. Besides training his "Ironsides," he organized parliament in 1653. He had beaten the King's forces, and made himself master of England. His reign caused England to be respected and honored abroad, but it was not popular at home. He died in 1659 on the anniversary of his famous battles of Dunbar and Worcester.
72. [a.] The Parliament which Charles I. called together, sat for thirteen years—1640-53, and was really not dissolved for twenty years, 1660. [b.] The Parliament which Charles I. called in order to get "shipmoney." It met April 13, 1640, and only sat two days, being dissolved by the King.
73. It occurred in 1660 when Richard, the son of Oliver Cromwell resigned the Protectorate, and General Monk of Scotland marched to London, and under his protection the "Long Parliament," discharged by Cromwell, met and issued writs of election for a new one, and dissolved itself. The new parliament met and proclaimed Charles II. King.
74. Some of the Catholics being much persecuted under James I.'s reign, headed by Guy Fawkes, hid thirty-six barrels of gunpowder beneath fagots of fire-

wood, and it was supposed that they intended to blow up parliament. A discovery was made in time to avert the calamity.—1605.
75. a. Royalists and Parliamentarians; b. Tories and Whigs; Conservatives and Liberals.
76. It was translated in 1611 in the reign of James I.
77. *Upon the death of James II., 1688, his son, James III., desired the crown and was styled the "Old Pretender," and this *son's* son—Charles III.—was termed "Young Pretender."
78. Because of the fact that the "Revolution of 1688-9" brought William of Orange, who had married Mary, a daughter of James II. to the throne. She was older than young James and they changed the law of succession so it would put a Protestant on the throne. In 1745, the "Young Pretender" was defeated at Culloden Moor, and the Stuarts were never heard of again.
79. After the French and Indian War in 1763, the English troops were stationed in America to protect Canada from again falling into the hands of the French. These troops were to be supported by the Americans and added to this was the great taxation placed upon the colonies by the mother country. The people south of Canada, under the leadership of Washington, assisted by the French, gained their independence, and became United States of America. The Treaty at Paris of 1783 closed the war and England acknowledged the country to be free.
80. His brother William IV—1830-37.
81. †In 1884, Czar Nicholas of Russia attempted to capture some Turkish territory on the pretext of aiding the Greek Christians to obtain certain holy places in Jerusalem. England and France became allies of Turkey, and laid siege to Sebastopol in the Crimea. In the battles of Balaklava, and Inkerman, they

*Read Lochiel's Warning by Thomas Campbell
†Read Tennyson's "Charge of the Light Brigade."

worsted the Russians so much that they begged for peace, relinquishing all the territory conquered on the Danube.—1856. The East India Company began to settle India in 1612.

82. The native soldiers in the English service in India revolted because their cartridges were greased, as this was an insult to their religion. The massacres of Delhi, Cawnpore and Lucknow followed. The English succeeded in quelling the mutiny in 1859, and the East India Company turned the affairs of government over to the Queen, who in 1876 took the title of "Empress of India."

83. He was born in 1738, and was made Governor General of India. To meet the expenses of a war carried on against Hyder Ali, a Mohammedan warrior, in 1780, he expelled a rich native King of Benares from his dominion and confiscated his revenues. He afterwards resigned his office; was tried on the charge of malfeasance in office; acquitted at the trial; and granted a pension of $20,000 per year. He died in 1818.

84. The famous orator Edmund Burke.

85. It was colonized by English convicts in 1788 at Sydney. Gold was discovered in 1851, and immigration poured in rapidly until there were soon eight colonies all subject to England. Australia and the neighboring islands of New Zealand, Tasmania and the Fijis have all acknowledged Queen Victoria as their sovereign. They are now 3,388,000 square miles in extent and have a population of 3,500,000 souls.

86. The "*Impressment* of American Seamen," and the "Right of Search" *to get* them as practiced by the English. French Jealousies.

87. See p. 72.

88. William E. Gladstone.

89. 1837.

90. Lord Salisbury.

91. "No power can exterminate the seeds of liberty when generated in the blood of brave men."

Errata.

Page	10.	Byzanitum	should be	Byzantium.
"	21.	Overthrow	" "	overthrows.
"	23.	God, Good	" "	God of Good.
"	26.	Arbella	" "	Arbela.
"	29.	Dionysus	" "	Dionysius.
"	31.	Sophodes	" "	Sophocles.
"		Themistodes	" "	Themistocles.
"	32.	Russia [12]	" "	Prussia.
"	33.	Umbr-aus	" "	Umbrians.
"		Sabeins	" "	Sabines.
"		Tarquin the Proud—one King omitted.		
"	34.	Benevutum	should be	Beneventum.
"		Tiebia	" "	Trebia.
"		Caunae	" "	Cannae.
"	40.	Planutus	" "	Plautus.
"	48.	Bufus	" "	Rufus.
"	53.	Latfu	" "	Latin.
"	56.	War [1-4]	" "	Wars.
"	59.	1358	" "	1558.
"	70.	Bazane	" "	Bazaine.
"	78.	Bleuhem	" "	Blenheim.
"	80.	15th	" "	18th.
"	88.	bids [125]	" "	birds.
"	92.	bccame [48]	" "	became.

www.ingramcontent.com/pod-product-compliance
Lightning Source LLC
Chambersburg PA
CBHW022139160426
43197CB00009B/1354